Blood a[...]
Sermons on the Old Testament

To Norm and Sue

- Remembering our long friendship
- Grateful for our shared faith!

Michael Kathring

+ PENTECOST SEASON +
2014

Blood and Life:
Sermons on the Old Testament

Michael Kasting

http://www.bokstandpublishing.com

Published by
Bookstand Publishing
Morgan Hill, CA
4094_3

ISBN: 978-1-61863-787-1

Printed in the United States of America

PREFACE

Christian preachers come to the homiletical task in various ways. Some preach on a chosen topic, like marriage or stewardship. Others select a Bible text as the foundation for the message. In some denominations the sermon is a lengthy Bible study, often carried through an entire book, chapter by chapter. Lutheran preaching, by way of contrast, is primarily the proclamation of the Gospel of Jesus Christ as drawn from a biblical text.

Most Lutheran pastors base their sermons on appointed lessons from the church's lectionaries. In my forty-plus years of ministry, I have attempted to preach equally from the appointed lectionary texts – Old Testament Lessons, Epistles, and Gospels, and also from the Psalms, since there is a psalm for each Sunday and feast day as well.

The Old Testament, though it comprises the vast bulk of Holy Scripture, has suffered neglect from us preachers, possibly because it is more difficult to mine the treasure of the Good News of Jesus from texts that do not explicitly mention Him. The earliest preaching of the church, of course, employed the Old Testament exclusively in the decades before the New Testament books were written. There is more than adequate resource there for every preacher! One of my seminary professors said, memorably: "The Old Testament is the New Testament concealed; the New Testament is the Old Testament revealed."

Each of the sermons in this book is based on a text from the Old Testament. There has been a conscious effort to let the text dictate what is to be preached, lest 'text' become a mere 'pretext' for my favorite topics.

The sermons in this book were all preached during regular worship gatherings. I have endeavored to retain the format in which they were originally written, with notes included about where the biblical text is to be read. Words are often capitalized or underlined for emphasis, and I include directions about where interactions with the congregation (like a show of hands) are indicated. Direct citations from the Bible are in bold type.

The paragraphing style is borrowed from Peter Marshall, a book of whose sermons was given me by my aunt as a gift. His style has helped me in the delivery of these messages, and may help the reader 'hear' as well as 'see' the manuscript.

I express special gratitude to many who have blessed me in the preaching task. Dr. Richard Caemmerer, sainted homiletics professor at Concordia Seminary in St. Louis, provided a guide for outlining (goal, malady, means!). My vicarage supervisor and mentor, Pastor Winfred A. Schroeder, was both an effective model and an honest critic of my early work. Fellow pastors and my own parishioners have also provided insights and encouragement.

Is there a greater privilege for us humans than to be messengers of the grace of God in Jesus Christ? That gracious Word of God is the great burning fire at the heart of every true preacher's endeavors. "We cannot help speaking of the things we have seen and heard," said Peter (Acts 4:20). May that Word of God come alive for you once more in these sermons!

Table of Contents

THE RAINBOW SIGN
Genesis 9:8-17

The family was gathered again at the bedside
   in the trauma unit
   at Harborview Hospital in Seattle.

   They were keeping a lonely vigil over their son, who had suffered
   life-threatening injuries in a frightful auto crash.

   For days on end, he had breathed with the help of a ventilator.
   He had not moved, nor opened his eyes, nor spoken.
     "It could go either way," the doctor told his parents bluntly.

Then one Saturday evening, as his mother and father held his hand
and prayed with him, there came a tiny movement – his hand
squeezing theirs ever so slightly.

   They looked at his face and saw a tear at the corner of his eye.

   In that moment the mother and father embraced one another
     and wept joyful tears of their own.

     "It was a SIGN to me," said his mother, "a sign that told me he
     might come back to us, that there is still HOPE!"

We humans need such signs of HOPE in this disaster-filled world,
   where earthquakes rumble and hurricanes roar,
   where madmen's bullets and auto crashes end children's dreams,
   and where the greatest tragedy remains
     our human PERVERSITY and SIN.

   We need something that will lift our eyes, stir our spirits, and
   restore our faith.

How about you? Would you like a sign of hope?

Well then, child, look and listen, and I will give you one – a sign both
   ancient and enduring, and exquisitely beautiful –

   THE RAINBOW SIGN!

It came, the Bible tells us, right on the heels of the greatest of all
disasters in history –
   the flood that very nearly wiped the human race off the map.

   As the scene opens, we see eight people – Noah and his family.
      They have just emerged from the ark after spending a year and
      ten days cooped up with each other and all those smelly animals.

   Can you imagine the vision of devastation that met their eyes?
      The decaying bodies of the dead.
      The bloated carcasses of animals.
      The ruination of everything that comprised the civilized world.

      How would you feel if you discovered that your family
      was the only one left on earth...
         and the future was entirely in your hands?

"WHAT A MESS!" I can hear them saying. "Where do we go from
here?"

   Now comes God's answer: **READ THE TEXT**

A Rainbow! God gave them a rainbow!

   Not the sort of thing we've come to expect in the wake of a
   disaster.
      We're more accustomed to seeing
      the National Guard, hastily-erected tent shelters,
         and volunteers at the back of open semi-trailers,
         distributing distilled water and K-rations.

2

But since God is GOD and not the National Guard, Noah got something better - a RAINBOW.

That is to say, a RAINBOW SIGN.

A sign, first of all, to assure Noah that God was still there, even in the aftermath of disaster.

It's as if He were saying to Noah,
"I know you're overwhelmed. So stop and look UP.
Take heart. I'm here. And I am still at work."

Is that what you see when you look at a rainbow?
Or have we modern folks grown so jaded, so foggy in our vision, that to us a rainbow is nothing more than sunlight refracted on water?

If we knew how to look at life through God's eyes, wrote French priest Michel Quoist, *we would see it as innumerable tokens of the love of the Creator.*

Children know. They have not grown too old to see.

Many years ago our family had finished eating supper at a restaurant in Bend, Oregon.
We emerged just as the sun was setting. We stopped and looked appreciatively.
Our daughter, just a toddler, announced to us,
"God painted that!"

"Look," God said to Noah. "Just look at that. I painted it, and now I give it to you as a sign, so that you will not forget that I am here, and I am at work."

Ah, but WHAT WORK?

For life is complex and confusing,
   and even for us who are convinced there IS a God,
   there remains a lot of uncertainty about what He's up to.

   So listen further, for with the RAINBOW SIGN comes an
   explanation:
      This, God tells Noah, **is the sign of the covenant I make
      between me and the world, that never again will there be a
      flood to destroy the earth.**

Why did God choose a RAINBOW as the sign of His promise?
   Because it is a picture-word.

   The Hebrew word for RAINBOW
      is actually the word used everywhere else for a soldier's bow –
         one used to shoot arrows, to make WAR!

   The RAINBOW was a sign that God had made a decision.
      NEVER AGAIN! He said. I have hung up my bow!
      Never again will I use a flood.

      Never again will I respond to human sin
         with the sheer force of my anger.

      I WILL USE ANOTHER WAY!

God's decision reminds me of what a teacher might do with a
troublesome student.

   Perhaps the teacher has butted heads with a defiant child again and
   again. There are penalties, detentions, and even expulsions.

   But it isn't working. The student is still defiant.

   So the teacher decides, at some cost and risk, to try another
   approach. Decides to reach out with patience, extra listening,
   extra love.

4

The RAINBOW is a sign that God has decided to come at sin,
   not with FORCE, but with GRACE,
      letting His last word to us be undeserved KINDNESS,
         not the PUNISHMENT we had coming.

Not an easy decision for a just and holy God who hates sin!

So He puts the rainbow in the sky,
      not only to remind NOAH, but to remind HIMSELF!

   When the bow is in the clouds, he says,
   I will look upon it and remember.

Aren't you glad God keeps looking…and remembering?

   For if there were no RAINBOW SIGN,
      then every few generations there would have had to come
      yet another devastating punishment on this violent world.
         Another Flood. And then another!

   And if there had been no RAINBOW SIGN,
      then every time I sinned, or you did, we could expect some
      dread disease, some snakebite, some bolt of lightning in answer.

      None of us would have reached adulthood!
      Human life would be short and bitter, and all would soon end.

Ah, but there is no lightning bolt. There is instead a RAINBOW.
   Not because we haven't sinned,
   but because God has decided to be gracious.

As God unfolded His plan of Grace, the Rainbow Sign was followed by
other signs.

   For Abraham, it was CIRCUMCISION,
      the sign God had chosen Him and his descendants
      to be the vehicle of that covenant blessing.

For Moses and the Israelites, it was a
LAMB'S BLOOD ON THE DOOR,
    the sign that God would 'pass over' their houses
    and liberate them from slavery in Egypt.

Much later, to the shepherds on Bethlehem's hills, came a sign
announced by ANGELS:
    **This shall be a sign to you: you shall find a BABE wrapped in
    swaddling clothes and lying in a manger.**

That baby grew to manhood,
    and the astonishing things He did – the healing and feeding and
    making water into wine and the driving out of demons – were also
    called SIGNS –
       to open deaf ears and hard hearts and awaken FAITH.

And then, on a hill far away, came the clearest and most
gracious SIGN of all –
    that wooden cross, where God said finally and unmistakably,
    "I LOVE YOU" and "I FORGIVE YOU."

    There every sin's debt was fully paid,
    every stain washed clean by the blood of Jesus Christ.

Have you seen the signs? Got the message? Believed it?

Years ago, a farm boy from Iowa had a falling out with his parents.
    In anger he packed his things, left home, and enlisted in the
    army. He made no contact with his parents in the years that
    followed,
       and his own bitterness grew deep and hard.

Then came World War II, and that young man was thrown into the
horrors of death and destruction.
    His heart was changed.

Now, he realized, he wanted to come back home,
   but after the heartache and years of neglect,
   would his parents have him back?

If he were to travel home, he dreaded what he might find.

   Would they bar the door? Refuse him?
   Tell him never to come back?

   Too frightened to phone, he took pen in hand and wrote a letter.
   It said,
      Dear father and mother,
         I realize that I have not seen you or even communicated
      with you in years. I would like very much to come home, but I
      don't know how you will feel about that. I have bought a
      train ticket, and I will be coming home on August 12. If you
      have forgiven me, and if you still want me, please tie a
      white ribbon around the tree by the tracks. That will be my
      sign to come home. If I don't see anything, I will stay on the
      train, and you will not have to deal with me any more.

The day came, and the young man rode that train across the
broad fields of Iowa.
   As he went, his sense of dread grew. As he approached the
   town, he could not bear to look.

But he did not have to, for a moment later the conductor cried
out to the passengers,
   "WOULD YOU LOOK AT THAT! A WHOLE TREE COVERED IN
   WHITE RIBBONS!"

God has done that very thing.

He gives us not one sign only, but a whole TREE FULL of them...
every one saying that He chooses to be patient with a world that
has scorned Him, gracious to each one of us when we stumble
and fall.

7

How is it with you, my fearful friend?
   When you think sin is too awful and there must be a limit to God's
   love,
      look up and see the sign called the CROSS that says,
      GOD'S LOVE HAS NO LIMIT.

   And when you despair because it looks like death finally wins in the
   end and all we do is in vain,
      look up and see that EMPTY TOMB....a sure sign that
      GOD'S LOVE WILL CONQUER DEATH.

   And if you think all this is for somebody else and not you,
      remember the WATER OF YOUR BAPTISM,
      the sign in which God calls you by name and says,
      "YOU ARE MINE!"

"Just look!' Noah cried out to his family. "Just look at that rainbow!"

   There it was, big and bold and beautiful,
   hanging in the sky like a banner.

You there.

Come and stand beside old Noah.

   When you look at this twisted world
      and wonder how long things can go on before lightning strikes,
      look up and see the rainbow sign that says, GOD IS PATIENT!

   He is. He was. He will be.

Take heart as you look at THE RAINBOW SIGN.

TOO GOOD TO BE TRUE?
Genesis 18:10-14

_____

A few years ago
    an older woman my wife and I knew called us with some good
    news.

    "I won a contest," she said excitedly. "They sent me a letter.
        It's $10,000! As soon as I get the money, I am going to give it
        to the church."

I didn't say anything at first.
    Very honestly, I didn't believe it. It sounded too good to be true.

    And this woman, though a very kind-hearted person, had always
    struck me as extremely naïve.
        "Are you sure?" I asked.
        "Oh, yes!" she beamed.

GOOD NEWS, especially the spectacular kind, generates both kinds of
responses-
    the skepticism I was feeling
    and the trusting acceptance she demonstrated.

How about YOU?
    What's your reaction to the good news that reaches your ears?

    Are you a BELIEVER, or a DOUBTER?

The Old Testament lesson for today is the story of another old woman
who heard the best news a woman in her culture could hear.

    Her name is Sarah. Hear again a portion of her story:
        READ THE TEXT

By now, Sarah is an old woman, nearly 90 years old.

Her hair is grey, her skin leathery from years of living in the desert
sun.   And there is an emptiness in Sarah's life that nothing can fill.

True, she has a fine husband in Abraham,
and wealth beyond what most women have.

But she has no CHILD.
    And having no child, she feels she has no FUTURE.

There had been a time when hope was kindled.

She remembered the day Abraham had burst into the tent,
beaming and energized:
    "God is going to make of us a great nation, Sarah!" he had said.
    "Children, Sarah... children!"

But that had been years ago.   How many?
    Sarah stopped to count. 24 years now!
    And each year was a nail in the coffin of her hopes.

Today would be no different.

Sarah covered her emptiness with busyness.
    Three visitors had appeared, and Abraham had set everyone
    scurrying to fix them a meal.

Sarah had done her part.

Her work finished, she had nothing to do but wait.
    She was good at that – WAITING.

    It was the hottest part of the day, and Sarah stood out of sight
    behind the tent flap, listening idly to the men's talk outside as
    beads of sweat rolled down her neck.

And you, my friend, as you sit here in the tent on another Sunday morning,
    what are YOU waiting for?

    Are you a young person,
    waiting impatiently for the privileges that come with being OLDER?

    Are you alone, and waiting for a FRIEND?

    Are you financially strapped, waiting for a RAISE?

    Are you sick, waiting to be WELL?
        Bored, waiting for some NEW, something EXCITING?

Suddenly, Sarah's ears perk up. They are talking about her!
    Where is your wife Sarah? asks one of the strangers.
    "There in the tent," says Abraham.

The stranger continues.
    About this time next year, I will come back. He pauses.
    And Sarah your wife will have a son.

Behind the tent flap, Sarah's eyes grow wide.
    The PROMISE!
    The old promise that Abraham had brought her so many years ago,
        but sharpened now to a specific time...
            "Next year... NEXT YEAR ABOUT THIS TIME!"

You have heard <u>your</u> share of promises too, haven't you?
    Commercials on TV that offer miracle diets to make you slim and
    trim again.
        Computer dating services that promise to find you a friend,
        lover, soul-mate for life.
            Faith healers who say your cure is certain "if only your faith is
            strong enough."

11

It sounds like GOOD NEWS. All of it. Our hearts hunger to believe it.
   We could all use some good news. Here most of all!

      Here in this house of God, where we bring our deepest hungers
         and yearnings.
      Here most of all we need Good news, promises we can believe.

"It's too late for me," Sarah whispered to herself.
   A BABY?
   She looked down at her old woman's body – the wrinkled skin and
      sagging breasts.

   She thought about her ancient husband and his arthritic knees.
   She couldn't help herself. SHE LAUGHED!

      Not the merry laugh of joy, but a quiet, bitter laugh of disbelief.
         Years ago she had summoned up some hope, but not now.
         She wasn't born yesterday!

         Some things are just too good to be true, and this was one of
         them.

Isn't that how it ends with a lot of the good news that comes our way-
with a bitter laugh of disappointment?

   Sweet-talking con artists disappear with our money.
      Miracle diets bring only illusory results – the pounds come back.
         The healing we prayed for encounters a setback, and we begin
         to doubt our faith.

   I'm sorry to tell you that our lady friend was wrong.
      The letter she got about the contest was either a cruel hoax
      or a promotional gimmick.
         She didn't win anything at all, and is now a sadder and wiser
         woman.

Has it happened to you, as it happened to Sarah?

Have you stopped hoping, stopped believing,
even though it is GOD HIMSELF who stands outside your door
and speaks the promise to you?

Are you one of the embittered folks I've met who say to me,
"Oh, I used to believe all that,"
but who are now skeptics who can't even pray anymore?

There are some of them in our little town, I'm sure.
The DE-CHURCHED, they are called – people who used to belong,
used to sing and laugh with joy in God's house. But no more!

WILL YOU WIND UP AS ONE OF THEM?

But listen now. Sarah hears another word through the tent door.

Why did Sarah laugh? the Stranger asks Abraham.
Is anything too hard for the Lord?

For this Stranger is no stranger at all, but God Himself!
He knows her well – knows that she is standing there unseen
behind the tent door,
knows her heart's sadness, hears her disbelieving laughter.

He rebukes her gently, as if to say,
"I know you, Sarah, but do you know me?"
"I know your sadness. Do you know my power to help?"

"Ah, Sarah, some news is too good to be true.
But the news I bring is TRULY GOOD – for it is I WHO BRING IT,
AND NOTHING IS TOO HARD FOR ME."

Sarah's picture of God was too small. Is yours?

In his book entitled *YOUR GOD IS TOO SMALL*, J. B. Phillips writes:
> *Men and women are living, often without any faith in God...this is not because they are particularly wicked...but because they have not found with their adult minds a god big enough to account for life, big enough to command their...respect.*

What's your picture of God?

Do you suppose that He is some absentee landlord,
managing earth from some other galaxy – uninterested,
uncaring?

Learn what Sarah learned!
HE IS HERE, IN THE MIDST OF THIS WORLD.
He comes, often unexpected, always graciously, to bring a help
unlooked-for.

And we know it better than Sarah.

We know that when He came into our world in Bethlehem,
it was not just for an afternoon visit, but for a lifetime.

And to His startled followers, who had a too-small picture of God,
He said,
WITH GOD NOTHING SHALL BE IMPOSSIBLE.

Nothing impossible?

Does that sound too good to be true?

Then let me ask again what it is you hope for as you sit here this
morning?
Would you with that some old enmity might be healed, and that
you might be reconciled with someone estranged from you?
Is that too hard for God – to make enemies into friends?
Would that be too good to be true?

Isn't that what God did with Saul the Persecutor,
    when he met him on the Damascus Road and turned him into
    Paul the Friend of Jesus, the Missionary?

Is it too hard a thing for God to lift that burden of sin and guilt you
have been carrying-to set your heart free?
    Is that too good to be true?

Ah, not if He would take that load Himself and pay for it
    with His life before our very eyes, which very thing He did
    at Calvary!

That Cross of Jesus opened the door to the very heart of God.

Why are you persecuting me? Paul heard Him say,
    and in that moment he saw the amazing love Jesus was
        showing him, his bitterest enemy!

Such unexpected love that changed Saul changes us, doesn't it?

What do you think, Sarah?

What if I told you that death could be defeated-that those dear
ones you buried you will see again with tears of joy in your eyes?
    Would you say that's too good to be true?
        Too hard for God to do?

Ah, sister, ah brother,
    that is just what happened at the Grave in the Garden on that
    first Easter.

There Jesus rose to life and met his astonished followers, to let
them know that
    NOTHING IS TOO HARD FOR THE LORD!

We will not always understand His mysterious ways, any more than
we can understand the simplest workings of our everyday world.

15

Early in the 1800s, a workman who assisted the great chemist
Michael Faraday accidentally dropped an expensive silver goblet
   into an open vat of acid.

Before he could retrieve the goblet safely, the acid had dissolved
the silver.
   The poor man was in despair, but Faraday assured him, "All will
   be well."

In short order, Faraday added several other chemicals to the vat,
and the silver was precipitated, albeit in a formless mass.

Faraday then sent the mass of silver to a silversmith, along with a
detailed drawing of the goblet.

In less than a week, the goblet was returned remade, none the
worse for its strange metamorphosis.

Faraday's assurance to his workman was not "too good to be true,"
   because his knowledge was great enough to solve the man's
   problem.

If it was not too hard for Michael Faraday to restore the goblet,
then it is not too hard for the Lord God
   to heal a sickness
      to forgive the sin,
         to raise the body from death – things we think are
         TOO GOOD TO BE TRUE.

We leave Sarah, but not as we found her.

One more year she waited, but this time it was hopeful waiting,
   for she had met in person the God who was
   big enough to keep His promise to her.

And when the baby came (and come he did!)
there seemed no more fitting name to give him than

16

ISAAC – which means 'laughter.'

For God in His mercy had given her a new and wonderful kind of laughter.

How are you doing in your waiting these days?

Let yours be a hopeful, joyful waiting, like Sarah's.

For God has promised that, no matter what happens,
    you and He will share the last laugh,
    for the promises He makes you are both GOOD and TRUE!

IN THE RIGHT PLACE... AT THE RIGHT TIME
Genesis 45:3-8

READ THE TEXT

A certain man who had never been deer hunting before
drove into the woods,
   got out of his car,
      and sat down on a stump 50 feet away.

   No more than 5 minutes later, a large white-tailed buck
      stepped out of the brush into plain view.

   That inexperienced hunter raised his rifle and fired.
      He bagged what turned out to be a trophy animal,
      the biggest buck ever shot in that state!

   Later when interviewed by the local newspaper,
   the only way he could account for his success was to say,
      "I guess I was just in the right place at the right time."

The Old Testament lesson I just read tells the story of JOSEPH,
   a man whose success could also be described that way –
      as being in the right place at the right time.

   When we meet him here in Genesis 45, he's in the RIGHT PLACE –
      in a position of authority as Pharaoh's chief assistant.

   He's come at the RIGHT TIME –
      just in time to head off starvation for countless thousands who
      would have died in a prolonged famine.

   He's a headliner. A difference-maker!

You would never have guessed it by the way his story started.
   In fact, for 13 long years, things could hardly have been worse!

   Just a few chapters earlier in Genesis,
      we meet him as a pampered teenager.

   He is doted on and favored by his father Jacob,
      which earns him the lasting hatred of his older stepbrothers.

   One day Joseph shows up at the WRONG PLACE
   and at the very WORST TIME,
      when daddy isn't there to protect him.

      His brothers sell him to slave traders,
      who cart him away hundreds of miles south.

   The brothers concoct a whopping lie about Joseph's disappearance
      and deceive their father, who gives him up for dead.

Sound BAD? It gets WORSE!

   Joseph is made the household slave for a wealthy man named
   Potiphar,
      an absentee husband whose wife is just plain bored.

   One day, Joseph shows up at the WRONG PLACE
   at the WRONG TIME.
      Potiphar's wife tries to seduce him.

      He refuses, as a godly man should, but his reward is to be falsely
      accused of rape.

      His furious master doesn't wait for explanations.
         He has Joseph thrown into jail and left there to rot.

It seems the only RIGHT thing in this terribly WRONG sequence of
events is that young Joseph has held on to his FAITH.

Yet that FAITH must sit in jail and wait, year after gloomy year.

That's Joseph's story – or at least part of it.

HOW ABOUT YOUR STORY?

Was your childhood home a safe and harmonious one?
Were you well-loved? Emotionally stable?
Has your life been a sequence of well-ordered events that fit
together and made perfect sense?

Or did you spring from tangled roots –
with a family at times dysfunctional,
and a life that was a disconnected jumble,
a puzzle hard to assemble or even comprehend?

Are you a JOSEPH, rejected by some you hoped would love you?
Wrongly accused?
Adrift with a belly full of bitter memories?

Or are you, perhaps, one of those brothers,
sitting on the shameful memory of a terrible wrong you did,
unable to confess it to any one,
but unable to forget it either?

As a pastor, I am witness to literally hundreds of human stories, many
of them confusing, some downright heart-breaking.

Let me mention two of them.

I knew a man caught in a downward spiral of alcohol abuse,
whose first marriage had broken apart and whose second was
shaky... who then had a wreck that left him paralyzed from the
neck down.

I knew a woman who was abandoned by her philandering husband,
who went through years of grief.

Then, just as she and her husband were reconciling,
    she was diagnosed with terminal cancer.

The families wondered, and I wondered too,
    "What GOOD can possibly come out of all THIS?"

    Have you been blind-sided by something?
        Felt caught in the WRONG PLACE at the WRONG TIME?
        Concluded that life doesn't make any sense?

If so, remember that Joseph's story did not end in that jail.

For his story, and your story, is also GOD'S STORY.
    Like a patient quilter, God takes the scattered pieces of our lives,
    even the darkest ones,
        and stitches them together.

In God's design, Egypt was not the WRONG place for Joseph,
but the RIGHT place —
    a nation whose fields could produce
    enough grain to feed a hungry world.

In God's design, that jail was not the WRONG place,
but the RIGHT one,
    for just there, Joseph was to meet Pharaoh's butler
    and interpret his troubled dream...
        and that same butler would tell Pharaoh, who had dreams of
        his own.

In God's design, it was just the RIGHT TIME,
    for that meeting with Pharaoh came just a few years before a
    disastrous famine,
        and Joseph was the one man with the wisdom
        to make a workable plan
            for storing the grain and rationing it in the lean years.

What seemed so WRONG turned out to be just RIGHT... in God's
Master Plan.

In the end, because of that plan,
Joseph saved the lives of many people,
including the lives of his father and brothers in faraway Canaan,
who made their desperate trip to Egypt to stand in line
for their ration of food.

God knew what He was doing, though neither Joseph,
nor his brothers,
nor his aging, grief-stricken father had a clue.

In the movie THE KARATE KID,
a boy asks an old karate master to teach him karate
so he can defend himself against some larger, meaner boys.

The old man agrees.
But the boy's excitement turns to disappointment
when the old man assigns him some meaningless household
chores.
He must sand the floor and paint the fence day after day in
the hot sun.
Boredom! Monotony!

He can see no reason, no purpose in any of it.
He wants to quit, thinking he has come to the WRONG PLACE
and asked the WRONG PERSON.

But the wise karate master has his own plan.
Through the repeated sanding and painting motions,
this hitherto weak and undisciplined boy
is learning the basic karate movements.

His body is being hardened and his skills sharpened all the time,
though he does not know it.

I have seen God, the Great MASTER, at work in lives –
even in the most puzzling, heart-breaking circumstances.

That alcoholic man I told you about, who was paralyzed in the accident,
was weaned off alcohol,
was brought back to a faith in God,
came back to his church,
and lived many productive years.

That woman, diagnosed with terminal cancer,
let the light of her faith shine on her back-slidden husband.

After her death, he also returned to his faith after years of disobedience.

Their daughters, strengthened in the ordeal,
became ardent believers
and have formed a Gospel-singing team who share
their faith through their music.

With God at work in a life, there are no WRONG TIMES that cannot be redeemed,
no WRONG PLACES that cannot witness the Master's working,
in spite of the tangles our human sin has left.

All things work together for good to those who love the Lord,
wrote Paul, a missionary who was jailed for his work.

Even under sentence of death and house arrest, he later
concluded that **what has happened to me has really served to advance the Gospel,**
as he made his witness even to the soldiers guarding him.

What about YOU, friend?

I can say with certainty that at this moment,

24

each of you is in the RIGHT PLACE,
and this is the RIGHT TIME.

How do I know?

Because this is the place where and the time when
God meets His people most directly,
    where His word of pardon and hope is spoken,
        where the body and blood of Jesus is offered to all who will
        receive it.

This wondrous love of God flows so freely because of someone else
who was at the RIGHT PLACE at the very RIGHT TIME.

Romans 5 says it simply, sweetly:
    **At the right time, Christ died for the ungodly... while we were
    yet sinners, Christ died for us.**

Like a JOSEPH sent to Egypt to save people dying from hunger,
Jesus was sent to a world starved for forgiveness and peace.

Like Joseph, someone else's sins forced Jesus to become a slave,
sold for 30 pieces of silver, cast away, given up for dead.

Yet through Him, as through Joseph,
God worked a MIGHTY DELIVERANCE.

Jesus was in just the RIGHT PLACE,
    for there at the cross he took my place, your place,
    so that we might have HIS PLACE –
        a place at the Father's table in the heavenly banquet.

Where are you this morning?
    In what time of your life?
    In what circumstances, what state of mind?

Wherever you are, if your heart is open to receive the love of God in Jesus Christ,
   you are in the RIGHT PLACE.

And now is the RIGHT TIME to say
   "Yes, Lord. Come near to me
   and work your will in my life."

I PROMISE
Exodus 24:3-11

_____

READ THE TEXT

Just listen to them!
All that the Lord has spoken we will do!

Do you think they really mean it?
Have they any notion of the commitment
   to which they're binding themselves?

This isn't just a story in a book.   It's a page out of our daily lives.

The scene is repeated by people standing in front of this very altar –
people making BIG promises.

   A child is presented for BAPTISM.
      The pastor says, "It is your duty to teach this child the Ten
      Commandments... bring him to worship in God's house...
      Do you intend to do these things both gladly and willingly?"
         And the parents say, "Yes, oh YES!"

   A trembling group of teens stand for CONFIRMATION, robed in
   white.
      The pastor says, "Do you intend faithfully to conform all your
      life to the divine Word, to be faithful in the use of... the
      sacraments... and to...remain true to God... even to death?"
         And they promise, "Yes, oh YES!"

   A bride and groom process here for the WEDDING.
      Rings are placed on fingers. Right hands are joined. They
      speak the most solemn of human vows: "I do promise, before
      God and these witnesses, to be your loving and faithful
      husband... your loving and faithful wife, for better or worse...to
      love and to cherish till death do us part."

Their tearful eyes affirm it, "Yes, oh YES!"

Sometimes afterward I catch myself asking quietly, deep inside,
   "Do they have any idea what they promised?"

Not all promises, of course, are as solemn as that. Most are mundane
in the extreme:
   "I'll call you next week."
      "Your secret is safe with me."
         "I'll send you the money as soon as I get paid."

We humans are PROMISE-MAKERS.

Why do we do it?
   Because life is fragile.
   A promise is like a gossamer web that holds life together and gives
      it shape.

The nation Israel stood at the foot of Mount Sinai facing an uncertain
future.
   They owned not a square foot of real estate.
   They had no homes, no jobs, and no health insurance policies.
   They had burned their bridges to the past
      and had not even laid eyes on their future home.

   Spread out before them was a terrifying wilderness of sand and
   snakes and heat and thirst.

   Of those terrors, they had only a child's notion.
   But they had tasted FREEDOM, and they wanted more of it.

   Their confidence – yes, their cockiness – was high.
   So they made promises – BIG PROMISES!
      All that the Lord has spoken we will do! Yes, Oh yes!

You've said it. So have I.
   Bold promises. Uttered innocently, ignorantly...

before we entered the wilderness of thirst and emptiness
that is so often the stuff of daily life.

God knew all about what awaited them, and all about their human
weakness.
He knew what they had yet to learn:
when the dry times come and the wilderness oppresses,
we humans are PROMISE-BREAKERS.

And so, to impress the seriousness of His covenant upon them,
He required something more than words.

He required BLOOD.
Young bulls were sacrificed before that altar.
The blood of those bulls was drained into bowls.

We read,
Moses took the blood, sprinkled it on the people, and said,
This is the blood of the covenant that the Lord has made with
you in accordance with all these words.

The blood carried a warning:
GOD WILL HOLD YOU TO THESE PROMISES!
If you break them, blood will be required!

You know the rest of the story, the very sad story.
In spite of their words,
and even in spite of the blood sprinkled on them,
the people broke their promises to God.

They worshipped a golden calf.
They complained in the face of the miraculous food He
supplied.
They stood at the brink of the land He promised
and out of plain fear they mutinied and clamored to
return to Egypt.

Their story is ours.
How often we have broken the promises we so confidently uttered!

The promised phone call was never made.
That borrowed money never returned.
The secret we said we would keep slipped out and made its
way all over town.

HUMANS ARE PROMISE-BREAKERS.

Tune in any day of the week to Dr. Laura on the radio or Judge Judy
on TV, and watch the parade of promise-breakers file past.

We are in that parade, sad to say. All of us.

We, church people, also forget the words we speak.
We renege on our vows.

Half of the children baptized in church
are never enrolled in confirmation class.

Nearly half of the couples married at our altars wind up divorced.

And what of those white-robed confirmands?
I'm afraid to count how many of the young people I've
confirmed
have drifted away into the wilderness of the world.

Even the strongest and most sincere among us
have left a trail of tears and broken promises behind.

Some finally decide that promise-making is too costly, too
forbidding, so we avoid making commitments wherever possible.

Couples decide to live together rather than marrying.

A woman whose husband was headed out the door to a

meeting shouted after him,
"Whatever you do, don't SIGN anything!"

It would be a thoroughly depressing scene if not for the second party to this covenant in Exodus 24.

Half the blood, you remember, was sprinkled on the PEOPLE that day. But what about the rest?
The other half Moses sprinkled on the altar.

That is to say, on GOD!

God entered this covenant too. AND GOD IS A PROMISE-KEEPER!

The altar they built at the foot of the mountain was a visible symbol of God among them.

The blood on the altar was God saying,
"I bind myself to you, my people!"

The blood was the indelible ink
with which God promised to be faithful.

And FAITHFUL He was in those wilderness years that followed.

More amazing than the FAITHLESSNESS of fickle Israel
is the CONSTANCY of God,
whose heart was broken again and again,
who yet remembered the blood of the covenant He made.

Even when He grew angry with them,
He maintained the connection,
persistently pursued them
and kept welcoming back his adulterous nation.

God is like a boxer, beaten and bloodied, who refuses to be counted out, but staggers to his feet again and yet again.

If we are faithless, wrote Paul in amazement,
    he remains faithful.

When our debt of broken promises grew to mountainous proportions,
    He came down in person to PAY THEM ALL.

    It was the faithfulness of God to His promise
    that finally sent Jesus into this world.
        All God's promises find their YES in Him!

Jesus came with love for promise-breakers like you and me.
Came to pay what we owed.

    In one of the old Lenten hymns is the line
        The Master pays the debt His servants owe Him
        who would not know Him.

See Him standing before Pilate, a condemned man. Hear the shouts of
the crowd:
    His blood be on us and on our children!

And that is just what He does.
    He sheds the blood required by a broken covenant.
    He covers us with that blood – to pay every debt
        and wash us clean of every broken promise.

But there is even more.

At the end of the story in Exodus 24,
    God summons Moses and the leaders of the people up the
    mountain for a banquet.
        There on top of old Sinai **they saw God and ate and drank.**

In that scene we glimpse God's PURPOSE.
    He binds us in a covenant that He may bless us with
    lasting union to Himself and each other.

After our trek through life's wilderness, God intends
to bring us home at last
   and seat us at an endless feast.

At the Last Supper, Jesus re-enacted that ancient meal.
   This is my blood of the covenant, He told them, and handed them
   the cup to drink.

For all of us – his weak-willed troop of promise-breakers –
He left this meal, THIS HOLY COMMUNION,
   to be the place where His followers might gather even in
   wilderness times and let His covenant blood wash over us
      to mend broken promises and broken lives.

When you come to this meal, friend, it is a
'foretaste of the feast to come'
   where we shall eat and drink and SEE GOD WITH OUR OWN EYES.

The movie *PLACES IN THE HEART* tells a story mostly tragic.

   A young sheriff is short to death by a drunken black boy,
      who is then lynched by some clansmen.

   The sheriff's widow must carry on amid many hardships.
      Some in her family circle break their marriage vows.
      Acquaintances gang up to beat and intimidate her black
         worker.
      A merchant attempts to cheat her.

   At the end, however, comes a scene most strange and
   unexpected.

      It happens in a church, where worshippers are singing and
      Holy Communion is being shared.
         We see hands passing the bread and then the tray of wine.

   And then we see the faces.

There side by side sit the sheriff and the boy who shot him,
the husband who has cheated on his wife, and she at his side,
those clansmen and the black field hand they beat.

But now all harms are healed, and what was broken is
mended at last.

It is a picture of the feast to come,
a picture of what our faithful God is doing even now
in this holy meal to which He has invited us.

Because God is faithful, we may make promises without fear.

Our vows we confirm with a confident "Yes, with the help of God"
because we have seen Him keep His Word to us.

Come.

The table is ready.

PRAYER CHANGES THINGS
Exodus 32:7-14

_____

On a wall in my boyhood home in Indiana hung a plaque with a simple
message in gold letters:
PRAYER CHANGES THINGS

What do you think?
   Is that true?   Or is it a lot of churchy-style fluff?

Does praying really make a DIFFERENCE...
   or is it just a pious exercise
   that keeps us busy and quiet for a few minutes a day?

I know that many of you pray.
   So I invite you, just now, to take a few minutes to examine that
   practice and what you believe about it
      in the hope that your faith and your prayers will be
      strengthened.

Let me begin with a Bible story
   about a prayer that did in fact 'change things' in dramatic fashion...

   a prayer that literally CHANGED GOD'S MIND
      and saved 2 million people from sudden death!

It's recorded in the OT lesson for today – Exodus 32.

   Moses is on Mount Sinai, meeting with God.

      Far below, the Israelite horde is encamped,
      waiting with increasing impatience.
         Moses has been up there for 6 weeks!
         Maybe he's dead, they're thinking.

They have persuaded Aaron to make a new god –
one they can see – a GOLDEN CALF.

They start to sing and dance and have a feast.   Meanwhile...

READ THE TEXT

You'll agree, won't you, that this was a prayer that CHANGED THINGS?
Disaster was avoided.
The Israelites saved from death.

Because of what the Bible says here and in many other places, God's
people have SAID IT and SUNG IT and WRITTEN IT on plaques:

PRAYER CHANGES THINGS!

But WHAT, exactly, does prayer change?

The most common answer I hear is that prayer changes
THE PERSON WHO IS PRAYING!

Well, yes!
That is a healthy place to begin...

Get the log out of your own eye, Jesus counseled, **and then you
will see clearly to remove the speck from your brother's eye.**

So we pray God to change US, first of all.
"Lord, help me be patient with my children."
"Lord, help me control my temper, my tongue,
my bad habits."

Centuries ago, St. Francis summed it up in a now-famous prayer,
Lord, make me an instrument of your peace.

Over the years, God has done just so with many of us.

Early in my ministry, I found myself increasingly resentful
toward my secretary, who had grown critical and caustic
in her remarks to me.
   I prayed for God to help me understand her.

A few days later, as we talked about some ordinary office matters,
she suddenly began to cry, and proceeded to tell me about her
thoughtless husband and her wayward adult son.
   In that moment, I understood her pain, and my resentment
   melted away.

Most people would grant that much to our prayers.
   They will, at least, change us who are doing the praying.

But NO MORE THAN THAT, say the doubters.
   It's a good spiritual exercise, they say, like yoga!
   It makes you a better person – stronger, kinder, more faithful
      perhaps.

But what about our prayers for others?
   Moses, after all, wasn't praying for HIMSELF that day.
      He was praying for someone else.

That kind of prayer we call an INTERCESSION.
   INTER means 'between.' CEDE means 'step.'

Moses 'stepped between' an angry God and His sinful people,
   who had rebelled against God and made an idol to worship.

What Moses did was like stepping in front of a runaway locomotive
or a charging bull!
      It took courage... and love.

The Israelites didn't deserve it. They deserved to be destroyed.
   God had a right to destroy them.
      But Moses prayed anyway. He INTERCEDED.

It's what we do every Sunday here at church. The pastor stands at the altar – steps between God and people – and prays INTERCESSIONS.

For sick people to be healed.

For straying people to be found.

For people facing some decision to receive guidance.

For the grieving to be comforted.

The pastor isn't the only one doing this.
Many of you pray daily for others inside and outside the church.

Every Tuesday morning there is a small group of women who meet right here to pray for the requests you write on cards and put in the offering plate.

For years we have had an extremely active prayer chain –
many of you have been prayed for by that chain of intercessors.

What about those prayers...DO THEY CHANGE ANYTHING?

The resounding answer from the Bible is YES!
The prayer of a righteous man has great power in its effects,
wrote James.

The Red Sea parted.

Plagues were stopped.

Three men survived a fiery furnace.

Daniel was rescued from lions, and Peter from jail...
all because of prayer!

The resounding answer from centuries of Christian experience is YES.

A certain mother was anguished over her teenaged son.

The boy was a trouble-maker who roamed with a gang of other hoodlums. He was a persistent thief, a liar, and promiscuous as well. He had fathered a child out of wedlock.

38

Desperately the mother prayed, but for a long time it seemed nothing happened.

She went to her bishop for counsel. "Keep praying, and keep believing," he told her. "The child of so many prayers cannot perish."

His words came true.

The boy had an unexpected encounter with God one day in an orchard, where he chanced upon a copy of the Bible and began to read.

His life was changed, and he became, first, a believer, then a priest, and finally one of the great teachers of the church – a man we know as ST. AUGUSTINE.

For those who prefer scientific proof, there is even some of that! Recent tests, repeated in a number of places, confirm that hospital patients who are prayed for consistently

do better physically and emotionally than those who are not prayed for.

If you have, over years, practiced praying for others, you need no scientific studies.

You know. You have seen - and heard –
PRAYER CHANGES THINGS!

Not only the person PRAYING, but the person PRAYED FOR.

But the news I have for you this day is even better than that!

For if we take seriously this story in Exodus 32, we hear the most amazing truth of all.

Prayer may even change <u>God Himself!</u>

Did you hear the final verse I read a few minutes ago?

Then the Lord relented and did not bring on His people the disaster he had threatened.

The Hebrew word translated as 'relented' means
'to change one's mind.'

Is that possible?

Many of us have grown up with the notion that God's will is forever fixed –
    written in stone – unchangeable! How absurd, the critics say, to
    think that God might CHANGE HIS MIND
       because of what someone down here prays.

    But what if – here and there at least – God has deliberately left
    some things open – that is to say, left it to us to fill in the holes
    with our prayers
             (hold up paper with holes in it)
    like the holes in this piece of paper.

Why else would the Bible say, in James 4,
    You <u>have</u> not because you <u>ask</u> not?

Why else are we told this amazing story of Moses wrestling with God in prayer,
    and the incredible result: GOD RELENTED!

    That is a word of GRACE we desperately need to hear.

For it is not the Israelites only who rebelled against God and broke His great heart,
    not the Israelites only who deserved death and hell...
    WE HAVE SINNED TOO!
      We have turned every one to his own way

    WE DESERVED TO DIE!
      and God had passed His verdict – **the soul that sins shall die!**

40

Who would be our MOSES?
  Who would place Himself squarely in front of God and say,
    "Strike me, not them!"
    "Change your verdict – let them live!"

  There was such a man – a man like Moses. The man named Jesus,
    whom the Bible calls **The Mediator between God and men**.

  Jesus was the MAN IN THE MIDDLE
    who came to pray for us
    who came to change God's mind – God's verdict on us.

How He prayed!

The Bible tells us that Jesus was always headed off somewhere to pray
– even before the sun came up!

  He prayed for a whole day before choosing the 12.
    He prayed for Peter that his faith "not fail."
      He prayed for his executioners, **Father, forgive them.**

  And, yes, He prayed for US, his people,
    that we might be ONE, protected from the Devil, effectual in
    our witness.

Like Moses, Jesus stepped between…literally.
  He also did it on a mountain – not Sinai, but Calvary.

  There he was suspended on a cross between HEAVEN and EARTH
                or, more precisely,
  between a HOLY GOD and His UNHOLY PEOPLE

    Jesus offered Himself – and intercepted the judgment that was
    headed for us like a runaway freight train.

There, brothers and sisters, God changed His mind about you and me.

GUILTY no longer.   INNOCENT now!
HELL no longer our destination. HEAVEN instead.

History changed that day when God changed His mind.
   Life... and death... and everything... changed.
         PRAYER CHANGES THINGS!

The prayers of Jesus changed everything for you and me.
   For he was both the PRAYING ONE
                     and
               the ANSWER TO THAT PRAYER.

And He is praying still, the Bible says.
   Even at the right hand of the Father,
   He lives to make intercession for us.

Does it not embolden you to pray
   in those dark, empty moments when you wonder
      if there is a God at all,
      if there is any ear that listens to you?

He who died and rose for you now PRAYS for you

The prayer of a RIGHTEOUS MAN has great power.

That's JESUS, the Righteous Man whose sacrifice on Calvary
   put sinful people right with God
   and who, even now, prays that we may stay that way!

The prayer of a RIGHTEOUS MAN has great power.

That's YOU too!
   In Jesus, you are now, by grace, a RIGHTEOUS man or woman
   whose prayers have great effect!

You may indeed become His hands, His feet, His mouth as you pray,
   and YES, you may be an ANSWER to someone else's prayer with

42

God's help.

A certain priest, Father Bertram White, had long been interested in the work of a group of nuns in Calcutta, India.

He booked passage on a plane, flew to Calcutta, and without announcing himself, went one day to the missionary house to join in the mass.

At the door he was greeted by a nun he had never met. She took one look at him and said,
    "Thank God you're here, Father! Come in..."

Fr. White was incredulous, for he had told no one he was coming, and he was dressed in street clothes with no collar.
    "How did you know I was a priest?" he asked the nun.

    "Oh," she answered simply, "the priest who usually says our mass could not be here today, so we prayed this morning for God to send us another, and here you came."

What are you praying for, friend?

What are you praying for your COUNTRY in this time of frightful need?
    What are you praying for the CHURCH and its mission?
        What are you praying for this CONGREGATION?
            for the LOST?
                for the DYING?
                    for YOUSELF?

You can ask great things, you know.
    For Jesus has come, and because of Him,
    God has left some empty holes.

PRAY!

For PRAYER CHANGES THINGS!

BLOOD AND LIFE
Leviticus 17:11-14

_____

One thing about the Christian faith that shocks people
    and even repels some completely
    is all its talk about BLOOD.

BLOOD STAINS THE PAGES OF THE BIBLE.

    The blood of Abel, the first murder victim, cries to God from the
    ground.

    There are frightful, bloody wars.
        Goliath is beheaded,
          Asahel run through,
            Saul's dead body pinned to the wall at Beth-shan.

    The Temple is a vast slaughterhouse where thousands of
    sheep, goats, and cattle are sacrificed year after year.

    At the center of it all is the death of our Lord Jesus Himself,
    described in grisly detail, with a Roman spear puncturing his side
    and blood and water spilling out.

This morning, we will hear it again
    when we come to this altar to kneel down and hear the words,
        Take and drink, this is the true blood...

What are we to say to critics who dismiss the Christian faith
as a vestige of the Dark Ages
    or even to some of our own people put off by all this talk of blood?

There is a text in the Bible
    that is a DOORWAY to a different understanding of all this blood,
    even the blood of Jesus.

If we listen well, we will learn that blood is not simply stains and death, but something blessedly more.

READ THE TEXT

If you've thought of blood as DEATH, hear this word well:
BLOOD IS LIFE!
The life, says Leviticus, **is in the blood.**

A young man, uncertain of his medical vocation, was at work as an orderly one night in a London hospital.
Uncertain he was because the sight of blood had always made him queasy.
How could he become a doctor if he couldn't stand the sight of blood?

That night everything would change.
A young woman, injured in an auto accident, was wheeled into the E.R. Loss of blood had turned her deathly white.
Oxygen starvation had shut down her brain into unconsciousness.

The staff sprang into action.
One nurse raced to get bags of blood.
Another removed the woman's clothing.
A doctor set up the transfusion apparatus.
Meanwhile, the orderly tried to take her pulse, but found none. He was sure she was dead.

Then the nurse arrived with the blood, and the bag was attached to the pole
while the doctor punctured the woman's vein with a needle.

The orderly would never forget what happened next...
A spot of pink appeared, like a drop of watercolor, on her cheek.
Then it began to spread.
Her face flushed red, lips darkened, and her body quivered.

Moments later, her eyelids fluttered open.

She looked at the startled orderly and asked for water.

I felt I had seen a MIRACLE, he later recalled, *a corpse resurrected... the creation of Eve when breath entered and animated her body. I never saw blood the same way again.*

Not DEATH, but LIFE, is what blood is about!

And each of you sitting here this morning has that same miraculous liquid inside you.

> The average person has 5-6 quarts of blood
> flowing through 60,000 miles of blood vessels,
> some only 1/3 the size of a human hair.

> It is a veritable river of life carrying oxygen, calcium, amino acids,
> sugars, hormones, and more – feeding and servicing
> every one of the 120 trillion cells in your body!

BLOOD IS LIFE!

Can we begin to understand why God forbade the Israelites
to drink the blood of sacrificial animals?

> In the sacrifice, the animal's life was substituted
> for the sinful human who offered it.
> The blood was poured out as a way of saying,
> "We give this life back to you, God."

> Over and over it happened, because animals were, at best, only a
> temporary payment against the great debt of sin that was owed.

But then came Jesus Christ, the great Sacrifice to end all sacrifices.

> Once and for all, this perfect Lamb of God shed His blood –

that is to say, gave His life in payment of our sin-debt.

After all those centuries,
   the sacrificing of animals was suddenly ended.

And after centuries of hearing "Don't drink the blood,"
   God's people hear something dramatically new:

DRINK OF IT, ALL OF YOU!
THIS IS MY BLOOD OF THE COVENANT.

When we kneel at the Communion rail, this life of HIS is given to US.
   It enters, it transfuses us,
      like the blood that entered the young woman in that London
      hospital,
         to bring us His very life.

BLOOD IS LIFE. It feeds and nourishes.

But it does more! It CLEANSES.
   In Leviticus there are provisions for applying blood to priestly
   garments, to lepers, and to contaminated houses,
      all for the purpose of making them RITUALLY CLEAN.

   In Revelation 7 we meet the saints who have
   washed their robes and made them white in the blood of the
   Lamb.

   We sing a hymn that says,
      There is a fountain filled with blood drawn from Emmanuel's
         veins
      And sinners plunged beneath that flood lose all their guilty stains.

But wait!

Isn't that backwards?
   Blood doesn't <u>remove</u> stains. It <u>makes</u> a stain, doesn't it?

48

Detergent commercials promise to get out the tough stains,
and one of those is blood.

Remember Lady Macbeth, trying desperately to remove the blood
that stains her hand from murder?

Which is it? A stain… or a stain remover?

Think of blood where it was originally put by God -
inside the body.

There, most certainly, blood is a CLEANSER, a stain REMOVER.

The red blood cells which bring food to your body have another
task – the removal of waste gases, spent chemicals, and worn-out
cells.
All this must happen constantly, for some of these chemicals are
toxic. They would kill the body if not removed.

You would feel it demonstrated if you applied a tourniquet to
your arm, cutting off the circulation, and then tried to do simple
tasks.
Soon the pain would be so excruciating you'd have to stop.

But if you then released the tourniquet, a flush of blood would
melt the pain away as the toxins were removed!

So it is with sin.

Sin is not merely the breaking of a rule.
It is the release of a frightful power in a life –
a TOXIN that gradually paralyzes and finally kills.

Against that toxin, God sends the BLOOD of Jesus, the great
CLEANSER.
It is **for atonement,** says Leviticus.
Atonement means 'cover' or 'wash off.'

Not our <u>clothes</u>, but our <u>lives</u>, need this washing!

Without the cleansing action of the blood, your body would die.
Without the shedding of blood, says Hebrews 9,
there is no forgiveness of sins.

There is in this picture Good News for those who feel stained beyond
help.

Aren't there times when we wonder about a particular sin,
a specially deep stain that won't come out?

If so, listen well:
The blood of Jesus, His Son, cleanses us from all sin.

Even the oldest, deepest stains yield to the blood of Jesus.

Just as our own blood is brought near each cell by tiny vessels,
His cleansing blood is brought near you by the vessel of this
Word, by the pipeline of this sacrament:
"TAKE AND DRINK THE BLOOD OF CHRIST, SHED FOR YOU..."
to cleanse you completely!

Blood is LIFE. Blood is a CLEANSER.

Now the final element of this astonishing picture.
Blood is a SOLDIER.

Into every one of our bodies comes an INVASION.
Even through the tiniest tear in the skin pours a horde of invaders —
bacteria and viruses which begin to multiply and seek to overwhelm
the body.

The human body's reaction to such an invasion is immediate.
The capillaries dilate to allow the blood's defenders to rush to
the site of the invasion.

The white blood cells, or lymphocytes, are the shock troops.
    During healthy times in your life, some 25 billion of these float
    in your bloodstream.
        Another 25 billion cling to vessel walls, waiting as if
        on call.

    When infection occurs, many billions more are summoned
    from reserves in the bone marrow.
        The WAR IS ON!

The Bible says there has been an INVASION.
    The Invader who first snared Adam and Eve in Eden is still at work –
    in every church, every home, every single life.

    Satan is an invader far beyond our ability to resist,
        just as smallpox was a disease that once overwhelmed whole
        countries.

        There was little hope against it until Dr. Edward Jenner
        pioneered inoculation
            with a vaccine that gave hope against smallpox.

        He had discovered the power in the blood of a person who had
        smallpox, but recovered.

            That person's blood was called 'The Blood of an Overcomer.'
            When given in serum form to a new person,
                that inoculated person was said to have received
                'wise blood' that could resist the disease.

Isn't that what Jesus did?

He caught our disease – took our sin upon Himself.
    He let Himself be afflicted and suffered death.
    But on Easter He rose victorious... he became THE OVERCOMER!

    Now we who receive His 'wise blood' have not only forgiveness,

51

but the power to overcome our dread invader.

Jenner's serum worked.
 As inoculations spread, the scourge of smallpox retreated.

 Within the past century it has been totally eradicated.
 The last known case of smallpox occurred in 1977 after a massive
 campaign by the World Health Organization.

We have a similar confidence in the face of this spiritual invasion!
 It shall be defeated.

 The Book of Revelation, looking ahead with hope, says,
 They have overcome Him by the blood of the Lamb.

 When you share the message of Jesus, you bring that wondrous
 Blood to others who need it.

How do you feel about BLOOD now?
Indeed, how else could one feel after discovering that blood brings
 LIFE, CLEANSING, and VICTORY?

 Dr. Paul Brand said,
 I feel like assembling all my blood cells
 and singing them a hymn of praise!

I've a better idea.
 Shall we not sing a hymn of praise to Him who created blood,
 and who shed His blood for us?

 Let's do it now!

 (Lead congregation in singing the hymn
 "Jesus, Thy Blood and Righteousness")

WHOLLY HOLY
Leviticus 19:1-2

_____

READ THE TEXT

This morning I intend to preach about a 4-letter word -
   a good word which leaves a bad taste in many a mouth.

   The word is HOLY.
   An old-fashioned word whose meaning is not well understood,
      even by church people.

Don't get me wrong. The word <u>does</u> get USED!
   "Holy Cow!" said baseball announcer Harry Caray at many a White
Sox game.
      Others say, "Holy Toledo!" or "Holy Moly!"
      without being very precise about what they mean.

   People take Holy Land Tours
      and rent _Monty Python and the Holy Grail_ video
      without having a clue what God intended when He gave us the
      word and told us that's what we were to aspire to be.
         You shall be HOLY!

HOLY. An ancient word. An important word.
   Worthy to be studied...and prayed about.
   A word worthy of a sermon!

   So let's go back to the book in which holiness is a central concern.

The Old Testament reading for this Sunday is from the Book of
Leviticus,
   from a 10-chapter chunk of that book called the Holiness Code.

   At least 5 times comes this stern command:
      BE HOLY, FOR I THE LORD YOUR GOD AM HOLY!

53

That God is HOLY, no one would argue.
 But what does it mean for PEOPLE to be holy?

To most folks, holy means 'pious' or 'super religious' or 'super good.'
 Holy people, we imagine, hang around churches a lot,
  chanting like monks,
   or murmuring quiet prayers by candlelight.

 Or else they are unusually good and dedicated people – like Mother
 Teresa or Martin Luther King Jr.
  Very good people - and very rare!

 For anyone to say, "I want to be HOLY" would probably make
 people stare and then frown disapprovingly.
  Saying one wants to be HOLY seems to imply a kind of moral
  one-upsmanship – not merely 'holy' but 'holier than thou!'

   No one likes people with that attitude!

But in fact the Hebrew word for holy means something else.

 Not pious. Not super good.
  But rather 'SET APART.'

A holy place is a place 'set apart' for some special use.

 Like this church building, set apart for worship and study of
 God's Word.
  And the spaces inside it, like this chancel, set apart for those
  who conduct worship.

  That's why we have this railing, and why we ask people not to
  come in here unless they are helping to lead.

 Likewise, a holy day is a day set apart from normal pursuits –
 a day meant to be different from other days.

54

The way Governor Bradford set aside a day for the Plymouth colonists to give thanks,
> or President Bush set aside a day following 9/11 as a national day of prayer.

HOLY PEOPLE, in the same way, are people 'set apart' for some special purpose.

> Let me demonstrate.
> (Call the names of 3 people to stand and come forward).

You three people were called out by me for a purpose - to illustrate the meaning of the word 'holy'!
> And you just did it! You were set apart, so that the rest of us could understand what 'holy' means.

> Thank you…you may sit down again.

God's intent was to call out a people who would have a special role in the world.
> The Greek word for 'church' even says it – *EK-KLEESIA* means 'the called-out' people.
> Called by God.
> Appointed as His representatives.
> Set apart for his service.

Holiness is not just a label, it's a way of LIFE.

> God does not want his people to be so heavenly-minded they are no earthly good!
> No, rather, HOLY people are to be USEFUL people.

> For ten chapters in Leviticus, God spells out the shape that service is to take.
> > **Separate yourselves**, He tells them, **from the practices of your pagan neighbors.**

To be USEFUL to God meant they were to STOP doing the things the Canaanites did:
>> stealing, cursing, and lying,
>> incest and witchcraft
>> the dreadful child sacrifices to Molech.

The Israelites were to stop being part of the PROBLEM, and start being part of the SOLUTION.

>Start living a new way, says Leviticus:
>> loving the neighbor as much as oneself (even enemies!)
>> staying sexually pure and faithful to the spouse
>> keeping Sabbaths and feast days.

In all these ways, He says, you will be a reflection of ME in the world. Truly useful!

>Here's how Peter summarizes it in his first letter: **You are...a holy nation, God's own people, that you may declare the wonderful deeds of Him who called you out of darkness into His marvelous light.**

In other words, HOLY PEOPLE are not to be identified by what they wear, or how they look, but by how they live.

They're DIFFERENT!
>Yet, though they live a different life, they do not boast about it, or make a show of it.
>>*Holy people,* said Dwight Moody, *are like Lighthouses. They do not fire off cannons to announce their presence. They simply SHINE.*

So <u>do we</u>?
>Do we SHINE?
>Are we DIFFERENT?

The great problem with the church today is not that we don't understand 'holy'
>but that we do not want to be holy.

At least not WHOLLY HOLY!

God's intent is that we set aside ALL of life – all time, all behavior, all thought – our whole selves for His service.

>What He gets from us instead is partial holiness - bits and pieces:
>>a bit of our time, a piece of our income,
>>a fraction of our conversation,
>>a symbolic gesture now and then...
>>>the partial obedience of partly-loyal people.

>Wives, how would you like it if your husband said,
>>"Honey, I really intend to love you and be faithful to you...
>>every Monday and Thursday"?

We give God only partial love, partial loyalty, partial holiness.

>For what we really want is not HOLINESS, but HAPPINESS --
>>"life, liberty, and the pursuit of property" as the original words
>>of the *Declaration of Independence* read.

We have come to church today, to be sure. But what is it we seek?
>Are we asking, "What is the will of God?" or "What's in it for me?"

>Writer Eugene Peterson says that most church members in America today are RELIGIOUS CONSUMERS
>>who demand satisfying religious experiences and spiritual warranties for the good life as we define it.

>In exchange for our minimal presence and token show of support, we expect God to guarantee us a long life,
>>>uninterrupted good health,
>>and a host of other unspoken perks.

We pastors have too often fallen in line and become ecclesiastical CEOs, corporate managers who strive to keep the customers happy (HAPPY, not HOLY!),
>but who have themselves forgotten how to pray
>and who peddle their own images instead of proclaiming the sobering Word of God.

Is it any wonder that so many people in our society have walked away from what they disdainfully call 'the institutional church'
>and drifted into air-brushed cult groups
>and home-made spiritualities?

What they see is a very mixed bag.
>To paraphrase the third article of the Creed:
>>*I believe in the Holy Spirit, the partly-holy Christian Church, the Communion of part-time saints and most-of-the-time sinners...*

Even we who KNOW our faith in God is genuine
>can see in ourselves a troubling mixture of weakness and sin and death.
>>We have surprising doubts.
>>>We succumb to juvenile temptations
>>>>We think shocking thoughts and utter shocking words.

Surely the HOLINESS of the church
>does not consist in the holiness we bring with us through that door!

It has another source.

Back to Leviticus once more.
>I read further in the Holiness Code and found something joyful and grace-filled.

Two chapters later it comes, not once but three times.
>Leviticus 21:8 **I the LORD am holy – I who make you holy**.

The HOLINESS of the church, and of you personally, comes from God.
It is a GIFT, not an ACCOMPLISHMENT.

The same God who calls us and sets us apart
also fits us for his service.

Someone once quipped that the church is
Not a country club for saints, but a hospital for sinners.

Yes, sinners!
For there are only two kinds of people in the world:
SINNERS WHO ARE FORGIVEN
and
SINNERS WHO AREN'T!

The church as a communion of saints is nothing more than a
fellowship of sick sinners who are being doctored by the Holy
Spirit, given the medicine of the Gospel of Jesus poured
into their ears as they hear the message preached
and into their mouths as they receive the sacrament

Jesus was **The HOLY ONE from God**
whose mission was to make us holy too.

He did that by making a great exchange –
taking our unholiness, our filthiness
and giving us in return His own perfect obedience.

So God became man, took to Himself all sinful flesh, and put it to
death on the cross.
And we take to ourselves the Lord Jesus, who gives us his
obedience and makes us alive by His resurrection from the dead.

Paul describes it in Ephesians 5:
**Christ loved the church and gave himself up for her, that he
might sanctify her, having cleansed her by the washing of
water with the Word, that He might present the church to**

59

himself in splendor...that she might be HOLY.

The holiness of the church is a daily gift for those who have trusted in Him.
   My HOLINESS consists in my connection to Jesus,
   and nothing else!

Because of Him, I may say it with certainty:
   there is in fact a HOLY PEOPLE in this world.

   In the third century AD, a man named Cyprian wrote a letter to his friend. He said,
   In the midst of a really bad world, I have found a... holy people.
   They have a joy and purpose better than anything in life. They
   are persecuted, but they do not care. These people, Donatus, are
   the Christians... and I am one of them.

By God's grace, I too am one of them!
   Today, in His Word, He calls you to be one too.
   To live a 'holy' life in His service, as His instrument.

   Fling wide the portals of your heart!
   Make it a temple set apart
   From earthly use for heaven's employ
   Adorned with prayer and love and joy.
   So shall your Sovereign enter in
   And new and nobler life begin.
      To thee, O God, be praise
      For word and deed and grace!

The Rock that Gushed
Numbers 20:10-11

(The final sermon in a Lenten series on OT pictures of Christ)

_____

In northeast Portland near Concordia University there is a Pentecostal
Church with a memorable name –
> The Greater Solid Rock Church of God

That name comes from a hymn we have often sung here:
> *On Christ the solid Rock I stand*
> *All other ground is sinking sand*

A SOLID ROCK.

That's the picture of Jesus I share with you tonight.

> During Lent we are pondering Old Testament pictures
> that preview the redeeming work of our Lord Jesus, including
> > the Bread from Heaven
> > the Cup of Wrath
> > and the Silent Lamb.

Tonight the picture is a ROCK.

> But what kind of rock?
> And what sort of song would we sing to celebrate the truth
> in this picture?

> > Shall we proclaim Him a SOLID ROCK OF REFUGE in trouble
> > and sing "A Mighty Fortress is Our God"?

> > Shall we hold forth His teaching as a SOLID ROCK FOUNDATION
> > on which to build our lives
> > and sing "Built on the Rock the Church Doth Stand"?

Those are familiar pictures. Worthy pictures!

But NO.

Tonight I hold another sort of Rock before you.
    A picture strange and surprising. One we rarely consider:
        JESUS – THE ROCK THAT GUSHED.

    This picture also inspired a hymn:
        Rock of Ages, cleft for me,
        Let me hide myself in thee
        Let the water and the blood
        From thy riven side which flowed
        Be of sin the double cure,
        Cleanse me from its guilt and power

To understand both the picture and the hymn,
    you need to hear the STORY behind them.

It happened in the Sinai Wilderness,
    where the wandering Israelites faced a problem
    most desert travelers encounter – NO WATER!

As we join them tonight, the people are dying of thirst... and
    complaining.
        Why did you bring us to this terrible place?

    Moses is at the end of his patience, and angry!
        In desperation, he and brother Aaron prostrate themselves in
        the dirt before the Tent of Meeting.

    Now comes an instruction most surprising from God.
        he directs Moses and Aaron to assemble the grumbling horde
        at... A ROCK!

A ROCK? An unlikely spot to get a drink!
    Shouldn't he direct them to the nearest spring

or to some Bedouin well?

Instead God commands them to proceed to a nearby BOULDER.
   A big, hard, <u>dry</u> ROCK.

How often God does the unexpected, the unlikely…
the impossible!

Just months before He had done something similar.
   When the people needed a fast, dry road to escape the
   Egyptian army, God took them to the least likely place – the
   shore of the Red Sea,
      there to transform WET to DRY!

Now that they need WATER, He takes them to the driest place in
Sight,
      here to transform DRY to WET!

God often does things that way,
   for He must always be teaching us hard-headed people
   that with Him, NOTHING SHALL BE IMPOSSIBLE!

      Resurrection life from a bowl of water?
         Forgiveness of sins through bread and wine?
            God's very wisdom through the folly of frail human
            preaching?
      Well of course!

Just now in the desert what is wanted is some water.
   Water's what we want, Moses!   And we want it now!

No problem for God. The text tells us that after a moment's
consultation,
   **Moses … struck the rock twice with his staff. Water gushed
   out, and the community and their livestock drank.**

Nothing halfway about God's provision!

The water that came out was no mere trickle. Not a little dribble.
   NO!   The Bible says it GUSHED.

      Like a fire hydrant I saw opened on a Chicago street corner
      one muggy summer afternoon.
         The neighborhood kids flocked to it with exultant shouts!

There in the desert, that rock gushed water.
   Like an oil well exploding skyward... a crude oil gusher.

      Enough to satisfy thousands upon thousands of people,
      and all their cattle too!
         A river of water – FROM A ROCK!

Now turn your eyes to another place many miles and years away
   and see the scene repeated.

      There stands another man.   He too carries a long wooden ROD.

      He strikes a blow,
         plunges that rod, that SPEAR,
         into the belly of a man dead on a cross.

So John describes that vivid, horrifying scene.
And he should know, for he was there!
   One of the soldiers, John writes, **pierced his side with a spear,
   and at once there came out blood and water.**

Like the Rock in the desert, Jesus 'gushed' too. Blood and water.

   A doctor might give you a clinical description of this sign of death.
      A ruptured pericardium.
      The separation of red cells from plasma in His blood.

But for John, this was not simply a gory detail about death.
   For John and many who pondered the meaning of that Good Friday,
      there was something more to see in the blood and water

64

that issued from His side,
> something no less amazing than the water
>> that quenched the thirst of a multitude in the desert
>> and brought them LIFE.

For isn't that what Jesus has done, and is still doing day after day,
for thirsty people like us?

There came out blood.

BLOOD. John began to remember.
> **This is my blood of the covenant which is poured out for many**
> **for the forgiveness of sins. DRINK OF IT, ALL OF YOU!**

There came out…water.

WATER. John remembered what Jesus had said to the woman at
the well.
> **The water I shall give you will become a spring of water**
> **welling up to eternal life.**

St. Paul thought long over this picture too,
> and then wrote these astonishing words to the church in Corinth:
> **Our fathers drank the same supernatural drink.**
> **For they drank from the supernatural rock that followed them,**
> **And the rock was Christ.**

What God once did, He is still doing in this world.
> Thirsty, dying people came to a rock
> and had their thirst quenched there, though it seemed impossible.
>> They LIVED!

We too, thirsty and dying in our sins,
> are invited to come to Him who is our Rock,
> and drink, and bathe ourselves in that soul-renewing flood
>> that issues from His side.

From earliest centuries
Christian preachers and thinkers have seen here
a picture of the SACRAMENTS –
The Blood of the Holy Communion, and the cleansing water of
Baptism.

For both these acts, in God's mysterious working,
connect us to that Savior on the cross,
and that saving grace He pours out so abundantly
to quench and wash and restore us to life!
He has washed us in the tide
Flowing from His pierced side, Alleluia!

What do you do with a ROCK THAT GUSHES?

Well, what would you have done if you had been
among those parched, desperate Israelites?

I wouldn't have dallied more than a moment.
I imagine myself running forward,
splashing into that unexpected lake of water in the desert,
falling on all fours, drinking myself silly!

Maybe they did all that and more.
Maybe they rolled and bathed their dusty, leathery skin
in that delicious wetness.

And maybe, just maybe, they began to SING!

Come, friend, don't be SHY!
The Bible tells us, **Come and drink!**

Hear this message of a crucified and risen Savior.
DRINK IT IN! TAKE IT TO HEART!
That Rock of Ages was cleft for you too.
For your sins it will be a double cure that cleanses from sin's guilt
and power.

66

Drink it in.
Confess the sins.
Trust Him to wash you clean, even tonight!

It will make you want to sing.

That's what happened, you know,
at the GREATER SOLID ROCK CHURCH OF GOD in Portland, Oregon.

The people there got carried away one night.
Got so happy, like the children on the street corner in Chicago,
Sang so hard, sang so loud,
that neighbors called the police!

It happens sometimes when you stand in the middle of a miracle.
You forget yourself.
You sing for joy.

Let's do that right now.

For we are standing near to Him who is THE ROCK OF ALL AGES.
And the water's getting deeper!

THE SNAKE ON THE POLE
Numbers 21:8-9

_____

Most Christian church buildings have at least one, prominently
displayed, as if to invite passers-by,
> "LOOK! LOOK AT THIS!"

Our church has three new ones,
> planted firmly in cement bases behind our permanent sign out by
> the road.
>> You'll also find one on the front cover of every one of our
>> hymnals,
>>> another there behind the altar,
>>>> and a great big one over the back wall.

I'm speaking of the CROSS — the symbol of our Christian faith.

This morning I invite you to take another look at the old familiar cross
> from an unfamiliar vantage point.

> We must step back in time more than 1000 years before Jesus lived,
>> and we must step out into the desert — the suffocating heat of
>> Sinai
>>> there to behold...   (put up poster board picture)
>>> **A SNAKE ON A POLE**

Jesus Himself invited this comparison
> as he spoke one night with a man named Nicodemus.

> Hear his words in John 3:
>> **As Moses lifted up the serpent in the wilderness, so must the
>> Son of Man be lifted up, that whoever believes in Him may
>> have eternal life.**

Have a look at the snake on the pole this morning,

and as you do, listen to the story behind this picture.

The first people to see this sight were snake-bitten – literally!

The Israelites had been tramping through the desert for a long
time – nearly 40 years by now.

They were low on water, low on food, and lowest of all on
PATIENCE...

Satan had taken a bite out of their faith.
His venom had poisoned their relationship with God and
embittered their spirits.

Their words expressed their rebellious mood:
Why, they whined to Moses, **have you brought us to die in the
wilderness? There's no food, and no water, and we loathe this
worthless manna!**

Fiery words!
And God responded with a fiery punishment.

He sent snakes among them – fiery serpents they were called,
more because of their bite than because of their color.

They were poisonous snakes whose bite brought fiery pain
that spread and paralyzed their victims
and finally proved fatal.

A perfect picture of SIN at work.
A vivid depiction of the dreadful work of that ancient serpent
Satan.

Desperate and dying, they came in a panic to Moses, looking for
help.
We have sinned, they admitted. **Pray for us that God may
take away these snakes.**

Pause for a moment. Reflect on this scene.

Are you snake-bitten too?
  Has Satan slithered into your life and had his way with you?
  Have you griped, groaned, and complained as they did?

  Is your mind weighed down with some nagging worry so that
  your stomach is tied in knots and you can't sleep?

  Is your conscience troubled – harassing you with the
  remembrance of some old rebellion that separated you from
  God?

  Are you bitter, as if some poisonous venom were working its
  way through your veins?

HELP is needed, but WHERE TO FIND IT?

  If your car's low on GAS, you can look for Arco or Texaco.
  If you have a headache, you can turn in at the nearest
  Walgreen's for some aspirin...

But what if the trouble goes deeper?
  What if your heart, your mind, your spirit are poisoned with SIN'S
  VENOM?

  Then what?

In a large city years ago, a man went to visit a mental health
Counselor at a walk-in clinic.
  "I'm very depressed," the man admitted.

To every suggested remedy the counselor proposed, the man
simply gave a groan and said,
  "I've tried that. It doesn't work."

"Well," said the counselor, "maybe what you need is some healthy diversion – a good LAUGH! There's a show at the Roxy Theater – with a great clown."

The man looked up sadly. "I am that clown," he said.

When human resources prove fruitless, when inner strength runs out, WHERE CAN WE LOOK?

For the desperate, dying Israelites, Moses made his prayer to God, and here is the remedy God decreed...
The Lord said to Moses, 'Make a fiery serpent and set it on a pole, and everyone who is bitten, when he sees it, shall live.'

Moses obeyed. He fashioned a serpent made of bronze.
He set it on a pole, visible to everyone in camp...
and it worked!
Those who obeyed Moses and looked at the snake on the pole lived to tell about it.

A STRANGE REMEDY, you say?

Ah, friend, no stranger than what God asks us to do –
to turn our eyes on Jesus, hanging on a pole, to find our HEALING.

Stop a moment and compare these two:
THE SNAKE ON THE POLE
and
THE MAN ON THE CROSS

The one has much to teach us about the other.

Consider FIRST this simple fact:
the snake on the pole was something PEOPLE COULD SEE

Faith is a tall order for us humans because
GOD IS SPIRIT – we can't see Him, taste Him, or touch Him.

So to help us in our weakness, God gives us something we <u>can</u> see - something that reminds us of Him.

Moses did not bring the people a message in words only, but a MESSAGE IN WOOD AND METAL – something they could look at.

For us, God went one better.
He sent a MESSAGE IN FLESH AND BLOOD.
A living man who could be seen, touched, and heard.

That man was literally lifted up on a pole for many eyes to see, just as the snake on the pole was lifted up.

He who has seen me, Jesus assured, **has seen the Father.**

Consider, secondly, that what was on that pole
was not at all strange, but perfectly sensible!

It was a REMEDY
that perfectly matched and mirrored the PROBLEM...

A FIERY SERPENT TO HEAL
in answer to FIERY SERPENTS THAT KILLED

Isn't that how snakebite serum is made, after all?
A bit of the venom of real snakes is drawn, mixed, and then Injected back into the victim.

The VENOM itself becomes the CURE!

Now see what God puts on that cross!

If our problem is not SNAKES, but our own SINFUL HUMAN SELVES,
then what goes on that cross must MATCH –
a human being made sinful,
injected with the poison of all our sins.

73

Because He is human like us in every way, except without sin,
    He becomes the perfect anti-toxin.

On that tree he carries in His body the poison of our sins.
    In that way He becomes the SERUM OF SALVATION!

Consider, third, that God told the people to do something simple,
something
    incredibly easy:

Just LOOK! That's all.

JUST LOOK!

God didn't tell them to cross an ocean.
They can stay right where they are.

He did not give them some labor of Hercules.
    They didn't have to dismantle Mt. Sinai rock by rock,
        or dig the first Suez Canal with spoons!

        NO! Something SIMPLE. Just look at the snake on the pole.

God treats us that way too.

    Martin Luther said that if God had made salvation available
    only in a far-distant country,
        it would still be worth the huge expense of getting there.

    And if He commanded us to do some HARD TASK – like walking up a
    mile of steps on our knees – many people would attempt it,
        because there is nothing more important than
        SALVATION!

But God is MERCIFUL
    He does none of those things.
    What He bids us to do is simple in the extreme!

74

Just turn and LOOK! Fix your eyes on Jesus.
   Behold the Lamb of God who takes away the sins of the world.
   Look and LIVE!
      Believe on the Lord Jesus and you will be saved.
      Be washed – not in some rare perfume that sells for
      $100 an ounce – but in the simple water of Holy BAPTISM.

      What could be EASIER?
      Even the youngest and feeblest of us can manage those things!

God has made His grace as SIMPLE and AVAILABLE as looking at a
snake on a pole.

Will it work?
   Yes, but only for those who LOOK,
      who trust the promise of God spelled out here.

   God has put all His POWER and GRACE into this remedy.
      Now He invites us to come, to look, to be healed.

A few years ago, when my father died of cancer,
   I flew home to be with the family and attend his funeral service.

   I brought my grief along with me there, as many of you have done
   at such a time.

   I sat down beside my mother and looked at dad's
   funeral service bulletin.

      There on the cover were words of pure Gospel:
         LET US FIX OUR EYES ON JESUS.

      God ministered to my grief, and gave me a lasting peace
      as I let go of my dad.

Won't you do that today?

Bring whatever's eating you right to the foot of the cross.
    Look up at Him.
    See each sin, each shameful thought and act, nailed
        there with him, and hear Him say,
        "Father, forgive them!"

    FIX YOUR EYES ON THE CRUCIFIED JESUS.
    Find the healing that He brings.

Look long and trustingly at Him.

Soon you will see Him once more,
    now risen, living, looking at you with joy-filled eyes
    on Easter morning.

    FIX YOUR EYES ON THE RISEN JESUS.
    Find in Him the life that will never end.

REMEMBERING
Deuteronomy 26:5-10

In the early 1970s two young men returned to this country
after some harrowing experiences in the Viet Nam War.

The first was a PILOT.
He had been shot down over North Viet Nam, captured, and held
in prison for several years.
"I came close to losing my mind," he reported.
"The only way I held on to my sanity was by remembering
songs and verses from my Sunday School days."

The second man served in the INFANTRY.
He saw battles, blood, and death.
One of his buddies died in his arms.

After his return home, the memories haunted him.
He suffered nightmares,
went into a profound depression,
and eventually committed suicide.

Such is the power of our memories!

Some of us, like that imprisoned pilot, draw on our memories
for STRENGTH in trying times.
We remember the love in our childhood home,
the encouraging words of a respected coach,
the birth of our child,
or an answered prayer.

Others of us, like that infantryman, find our memories a source of
GUILT and BITTERNESS as we recall
an abusive parent,
the day we were fired from a job,

or an unexpected betrayal by someone we considered
a friend.

What sort of memories did you bring in the door with you this
morning?
    What are those memories doing to you?

We have gathered at church today for this very purpose –
    to help each other REMEMBER,
    and in that remembering to find hope and strength for living.

God Himself commands it:
    REMEMBER the Sabbath Day to keep it holy.
        REMEMBER your Creator in the days of your youth.
            Do this in REMEMBRANCE of me.

This morning's Old Testament lesson is another of the places where
God instructs our remembering.

    Here's the setting:
        The Israelites are about to enter Canaan where they will start a
        new life.

    When the first crop is planted, and the first harvest is cut, God
    tells them,
        each farmer is to take a bundle of produce to the priest at the
        tabernacle and say the following:

READ THE TEXT

"Start," God tells them, "by remembering WHO YOU ARE."

A goodly part of that remembering will be UNPLEASANT!
    A wandering Aramean was my father, and he went down into
    Egypt... there he became a nation...and the Egyptians treated us
    harshly, and afflicted us, and laid on us hard bondage.

Israel remembered, first, that it had been a nation afflicted and enslaved.

It sounds like Alex Haley's book *ROOTS*,
in which Haley recalls the terrible story of his ancestor Kunta Kinte, kidnapped from Africa,
dragged aboard a slave ship,
and sold into bondage in America.

We've been slaves too!

A significant part of our lives has reflected our bondage to sin,
a slavery into which we were born, and
reinforced day after day in habitual disobedience to God.

Remember, says this text. Remember who you WERE.
Remember the stupid, selfish, hurtful things you've said and done!

Maybe you say WHY?
Why remember THAT? Wouldn't it be better to FORGET?

The human brain can do that in some extreme circumstances, you know.
Certain blocks of time, certain painful experiences
can be erased from the conscious mind as a result of shock or trauma.

It's called AMNESIA.

Sometimes the forgetting happens for other reasons.
Medication can dull the memory. Disease can erase it too.

Years ago we lived across the street from a woman named Marie who was dying of cancer.

She had been more than a neighbor to us. She was also a friend who showed special kindness to our children.

Near the end, as she received increasing medication, she lost her memory.
> She forgot the long ordeal of her illness.
>> She did not remember who I WAS,
>> nor even who SHE WAS!

Although her amnesia brought a measure of PEACE,
> I remember feeling EMPTY inside,
> for she was no longer herself.

Some of us feel that's the best way to cope with painful memories.

"Just forget about it!" people advise each other.

Have you tried that?
> Tried to put out of your mind the people who hurt you,
> or your own embarrassing failures or shameful sins?

It's not easy.

Often those memories are simply submerged to a deeper level in your mind, from which they emerge again and again as nightmares,
> unexplainable depression,
> or even physical illness.

NO, says God.
> I want you to remember who you are, where you've been, and what has happened to you.

But don't stop there, so that you are left with guilt or bitterness.

Remember something more.

REMEMBER WHAT I HAVE DONE FOR YOU!

80

Then we cried to the Lord...and the Lord heard our affliction...and the Lord brought us out of Egypt...into this place.

More than anything else, the Israelites held on to the memory of how God had done that for them –
the miracle of the EXODUS.

Each Passover they retold it. Re-lived it.
He brought <u>us</u> out of Egypt... brought <u>us</u> into this place.

Not "them," did you notice, but "US"!

When I was a boy there was a TV show called *You Are There*, narrated by Walter Cronkite.
The viewer was taken back in history to
some great event...and through the eyes of the TV camera, he was invited IN to become PART OF IT.

In the same way, God invited the Israelites. "You are there!" He told them.
There at the Red Sea with your grandparents, watching the waters part!
"You are there" walking through on dry ground,
safe now on the other side,
no longer slaves, but a free people in your own land!

We Christians talk that way too.

We have come through deep waters and stand safe on the other side of Easter.

We too remember God's mighty acts of deliverance.
We recite them in our Creed:
I believe in Jesus Christ, His only Son, our Lord,
who was conceived by the Holy Spirit, born of the Virgin Mary
suffered under Pontius Pilate, was crucified, died, and
was buried, the third day he rose again...

Ah, friend, were you there when they crucified my Lord...
Were you there when they nailed him to the tree?

YES, we were!
During this Lenten season, that's where we're going again -
to stand beneath the cross with Mary and John,
look up into His face,
and remember those moments.

And WHY ALL THIS REMEMBERING?
Am I selling tickets for an ecclesiastical nostalgia trip?
Urging you to live in the past?

As an answer, let me take you back to the text in Deuteronomy.
After reciting all the past mercies of God, the worshipper is to say:
Behold, NOW I bring you the first of the fruit of the ground,
whereupon he sets his offering on the ground and rejoices before
the Lord.

The point is
Remembering the PAST
is designed to help us live in the PRESENT –
to rejoice in the NOW!

People who remember the mercy of God are enabled to do three
important things.

FIRST, they become generous givers to others.
I bring you the first of the fruit of the ground
the worshipper says to God.

And he means it, for He remembers: GOD IS MY PROVIDER!

In the early 1990s a citrus grower in Florida experienced a
devastating setback when a large portion of his crop froze in a
freak storm.

Nevertheless, he later gave a large gift – over $2 million – as a special offering to his church.

When asked about the timing of his extraordinary gift, he replied simply,
"It seemed to me a good time to remember all the good years that have gone before. I've learned that God will provide."

Will we take a moment this morning to stop and remember all the good years God has given us?

People who remember the mercy of God are helped to do a SECOND thing:
to have COURAGE in the face of trouble.

Is there anything that frightens me?
I stop to remember: HE DIVIDED THE SEA!
HE RAISED JESUS FROM DEATH!

John Chrysostom, a great Christian preacher in the early centuries, did something similar.

When the Empress Eudoxia threatened to imprison or banish him, he wrote a friend:
When I wonder if she will banish me, I remember that the earth is the Lord's. When I fear she will take away my goods, I remember Job, who said, 'Naked came I into the world, and naked must I return.' Will she stone me? I remember Stephen, and I take courage.

Facing some trial just now? Something fearful?
Stop and remember his word:
Nothing shall separate us from the love of God

and TAKE COURAGE!

Finally, remember the mercy of God encourages us to take our sins
to God and confess them boldly.

What enabled the Prodigal son to head for home?
Wasn't it the memory of how his father had always treated him?

Standing at the cross, we prodigal sons and daughters hear Jesus
say,
Father, forgive them. US!
And we find hope and peace again.

We ARE FORGIVEN. Now we too FORGIVE!

That's why you have been drawn here today, however it happened.
God was drawing you here – to come and remember Jesus Christ...
and to let that memory cleanse all the others.

Don't be afraid.

Unlock the closet door and let them all tumble out –
the painful, frightening, bitter memories
you've locked in there for so long.

Take them to the cross.

There remember that He loved you dearly,
and He will wash them clean.

A MOUNTAINTOP EXPERIENCE
Deuteronomy 34
(Preached on Transfiguration Day)

Sometimes I feel a desperate need to get away from the world -
   away from the traffic, the schedule, the ringing phone,
      away from the news stories about drug busts and global
     warming and the death toll in Iraq,
       away from pettiness and vulgarity and the prattle of
       politicians.

I get tired of it all.

Do you, as Southwest Airlines says, "Wanna get away?"

For me there is no better getaway than a trail that leads to a
mountaintop.

   Years ago when we lived in Washington State, our family took a trail
   to the top of Mt Townsend... an arduous climb, 3½ miles up from
   the trailhead.

   But when we got there, WHAT A VIEW!
     It seemed, on that lovely clear day, that the whole world was
     spread out in miniature below us.

   We could see the Kingdome in Seattle, 50 miles east,
       Submarine Base Bangor and the Hood Canal Bridge
       like a ribbon across the water,
        a tiny merchant ship far out on the Strait of Juan de Fuca,
    and, like giant sentinels on the horizon, Mt. Baker and Mt.
    Rainier keeping their ancient vigil.

How QUIET it was up there. How CLEAR!

Being there was a mountaintop experience that brought life back into perspective and helped us see again the greatness of God.

Do you need something like that just now?

Some of us are under tremendous pressure…
exhausted with the grind, anxious about a family member,
fearful about what this world's coming to or where life's headed.

Hear the invitation to lay it all down for a while.

Come with me, up to the mountaintop.
God has something to show us there, someone for us to meet.

Listen…
READ THE TEXT

You have met this man on the mountaintop before.

This is MOSES –
a man the Muslims call a prophet and the Jews call 'our teacher,'
a man painted by Rembrandt and sculpted into stone by Michelangelo,
a man Winston Churchill once called the greatest of human beings.

What's he doing up here, all alone atop this windblown rock called Mt. Nebo?

Ah, God has His reasons!
The first is to show Moses a GLORIOUS SIGHT:
And the Lord showed him all the land, says Deuteronomy.

Moses can see the blue sheen on the Dead Sea 3500 feet below
and the Jordan River valley winding northward from it like a green snake.
To the west are the rugged hills that ring Jerusalem.

Up north is the snowy height of Mt. Hermon, 70 miles
away, and the fertile fields near Megiddo.
Away to the south is the vast barrenness of
the Negev Desert.

Moses has never seen any of this until now!
For 40 years this land has been nothing but a promise from the
mouth of God,
a vision seen only by faith – the Promised Land.

Moses' whole life has been aimed at this place, and how often it
must have seemed an IMPOSSIBLE DREAM,
for first Pharaoh had refused to let the people go
then later Israel themselves had rebelled and demanded to
go back.

Moses had grown increasingly weary.
For 40 years he had pleaded and struggled and prayed,
always holding before the people the vision of the land.

Now at last – at LONG LAST! – it was coming true.
God had kept his promise. The people were poised to enter it.
The vision Moses had only seen by FAITH had now become SIGHT!

Do you have a sustaining VISION?
Something you see with the eyes of faith that energizes you to
keep working, keep praying, keep hoping
as you struggle through some desert years?

Martin Luther King had such a vision – of a land where people of
every color might have freedom and dignity.

That vision sustained him against the apathy of some and the
hostility of others.

In April of 1968, the night before he was assassinated,
King stood before a crowd of workers in Memphis, and spoke

in words that recalled Moses:

> *I have been to the mountaintop,* he said, *and I have looked over... I may not get there with you, but I have seen the glory of the Lord... thank God Almighty, we're free at last!*

Have you looked over?

Have you caught from God the vision of a dying world, enslaved and miserable,
   set 'free at last' by His mighty arm?

Can you hear the words uttered on another mountaintop:
Go and make disciples
   and know with a thrill that those words were spoken to YOU?

An adolescent boy in Philadelphia was touched by the Bible's command to feed the hungry. He envisioned himself doing that. So with his father's help, he began making weekly trips into the inner city to distribute sandwiches and coffee to the homeless.

A woman from Chicago named Ira Scudder was visiting her parents in India and saw desperation and death. She got a vision of a hospital that would dispense healing and hope. Twelve years later, after raising the money, she returned and built that hospital, and she was its first doctor!

We need VISION!
   Less TELEvision, and more MOUNTAINvision!

More people convinced that the Kingdom of God is an urgent matter, and willing to invest their time and energy for it!

But before we can have such VISION,
   we need something else that man on the mountaintop had -
   a close communion with GOD.

Isn't that why Moses was always climbing up mountains?

88

To be near God and hear His voice and seek His will!
Has there ever been a person to whom God came so close?
Think of their close encounters like
that first surprising meeting at the burning bush.

Take off your shoes!

There were the talks on Mt. Sinai – not for an hour only,
or even a day, but for 6 weeks, as Moses received the whole
law of God.

There was Moses kneeling in prayer, begging God not to destroy
the Israelites after they had made their Golden Calf.

When God talked, Moses listened.
Ah, yes, and when Moses talked, God listened!

Have you such communion with God? Do you seek it?

A mountaintop would be a fine place, surely, but one may have a
mountaintop experience with God anywhere.

Abraham Lincoln was spied by guests at the White House kneeling
beside his bed.

My wife's sainted grandmother communed with God on her porch,
reading her beloved devotional books and Bible in the morning sun.

A pastor friend of mine told me, "When I pray, I walk – away from
my books and my phone with the wind in my face."

Some men friends and I had a mountaintop experience with God in
that same Kingdome in Seattle I had seen from far away – over a
weekend with Promise Keepers.
55,000 men praying and singing to God together!

WHERE do you commune with God...and WHEN?

Sunday morning is a great place to start.
It's a mountaintop time for many of us!
In this sweet hour of prayer we commune with the Savior
who loves us and lifts the burdens off our shoulders.

But what of the days in between?

When, in each day, do you lay aside the distractions and open your
ears to what He's telling you?

Moses shows us the need for mountaintop closeness to God
to restore our balance and regain perspective.

But there's another reason Moses has come up here.
God has summoned him here to DIE.

The look he gets at the Promised Land will be his last:
I have let you see it with your eyes, God tells him,
but you shall not go over there.

Both Moses and God knew the reason for these stern words.

Months before, at Kadesh, the people had thirsted and complained.
God had directed Moses to provide water by speaking to a rock,
but Moses had disobeyed –
he lost his temper and his trust,
and he struck the rock instead.

**You did not believe in me, to sanctify me in the eyes of the
people,** God told him. **You will not enter the Promised Land.**

Even the greatest people FAIL.

Here on the mountaintop, in the presence of a holy God, we see most
clearly
how frail and sinful we are.

It is especially in those quiet times alone – whether on Mt. Townsend or alone in my room – that I come face to face with my humanity, my sin, my own great need.

Is that why so many of us have such a hard time with silence?

Is that why we surround ourselves with the noise of an I-Pod
    or the drone of a car radio
        or the busyness of the TV screen?

We fear what we may hear in the silence with God:
    "YOU HAVE SINNED...YOU SHALL DIE!"

But wait.

That was not the last thing Moses heard, nor even the last time he stood on a mountaintop with God.
    Was there not once more, and that one the best of all?

It was on a mountain high in Galilee, a mountain where he stood with Jesus Himself -
    The Mount of Transfiguration.

And here on that mountain we stand today, seeing these two connected in a special way.
    For what Moses began, Jesus finished.

Says John:
    The Law was given through Moses, but grace and truth came through Jesus Christ.

Look now at this other man – this greater MAN ON THE MOUNTAINTOP.
    Look at Jesus, who was like Moses in so many ways:
        saved from a bloodthirsty king as a baby
            sustained for 40 days without food
                radiant in face

a mighty intercessor for His people.

But how much greater He is!

   Moses shows what God expects, and how we fail.
   But Jesus shows how good God is to those who fail!

Look. The two of them are talking.

   We lean forward to listen.
      Are they discussing the Ten Commandments?
      The dramatic rescue at the Red Sea?

   NO, says Luke. They are speaking of Jesus,
      of **his departure** (his exodus!) **at Jerusalem**.

That too was on a MOUNTAINTOP –
   on Mt. Calvary, where the CROSS stood between heaven and earth,
   where we and God are brought close again,
      closer than even Moses was.

      For there on that mountaintop, sin was paid for.
         Moses' sin. And yours. And mine.

Those who have been to that mountaintop, and seen that Savior, need
have no fear any more of their sins, or their dying.

   The trip up the mountain to the cross
      is a trip out of the smog of the Valley of the Shadow of Death
      where we have spent so much time
         and wasted so much of life's energy.

   It is a trip into the clear air, where reigns our King of Mercy
      who wipes away the tears and fears
      and sets our hearts singing the song of the forgiven.

That's where Moses was going that day.

Watch him, now, climbing slowly, steadily upward in the morning light… toward the rocky heights above.

Moses knows where he is going, and why…but he does not fear, for God is there. Cecil Alexander described it this way:

> By Nebo's lonely mountain
>> On this side Jordan's wave
> In a vale in the land of Moab
>> There lies a lonely grave.
> But no man dug that sepulcher
>> And no man saw it e'er
> For the angels of God upturned the sod
>> And laid the dead man there.
>
> That was the grandest funeral
>> That ever passed on earth
> But no man heard the tramping feet
>> Or saw the train go forth
> Thus Moses, servant of the Lord
>> Laid down and found his rest
> And when he op'd again his eyes
>> He met his Savior blest!

So shall it be for all who know the Lord –
a closing of the eyes for a moment, and then that joyful waking…

If someone later today asks you,
   "Where have you been this morning?"
You may truthfully say,
      "On the mountaintop… and there I saw the Lord!"

CHOOSE!
Joshua 24:14-15

READ THE TEXT

"CHOOSE!" said Joshua.
>It was a challenging word for the Israelites,
>and an uncomfortable word for us.

CHOOSE!
>Day after day, like it or not, we must make choices.

>As soon as I open my eyes comes the first one:
>>Get up… or stay in my cozy bed?

>All right. I get up. Now more choices:
>>What to WEAR?
>>What to eat for BREAKFAST?
>>>Cheerios? Bacon and eggs? Last night's leftover pizza?

These are small choices. There are far greater ones.
>There's a job offer in Denver.
>>More pay, better health coverage, but it will mean uprooting
>>your family.
>>>Shall you take it… or stay put?

>>The new company wants a decision by next weekend.
>>You must CHOOSE!

A fellow asks a girl to marry him.
>They've dated for a year.
>She's head over heels about him, but she still has questions.

>>He wants an answer soon. "YES" or "NO"?
>>She must CHOOSE!

Such moments are forks in the road
   which will forever change the course of your life.

   We cannot go both ways. And we cannot go back!

"CHOOSE!" said Joshua.   But we'd rather WAIT.

   What's the hurry? There's always tomorrow…. ask me later!

"NO!" says Joshua.   It must happen NOW!
   Choose THIS DAY…

Some decisions cannot be postponed, because time finally runs out.

   That's the way it was on June 5, 1944.

   In a lonely room in England, Gen. Dwight D. Eisenhower,
   commander of the Allied Expeditionary Forces, paced the floor.
      He was faced with a fearsome decision.

   The invasion of Normandy was poised, awaiting his word.
      But he didn't know whether or not to proceed.
      Bad weather threatened the plans.

      If he said "GO" and the weather got worse, skies would be
      obscured for the planes,
         and heavy seas could swamp landing craft.

         The attack would falter, and thousands of lives would be
         wasted.

      If he said "WAIT," it would be weeks until the moon and tides
      would be right again.
         Precious time - and the element of surprise – would be lost.

   If only he had more time!
      But NO. He must decide NOW – this very night.

"Let's go," he said.

Joshua felt the same pressure. It was a crucial moment.

> The Israelites had taken possession of the Promised Land.
> One last time now they were all meeting before they scattered to
> their separate inheritances.

> Joshua was an old man. He knew he would have no other
> opportunity to speak to them like this.
> The moment must not slip away!

For some of you sitting here, crucial choices lie before you,
choices that will bring life-changing transitions.

> You HS graduates have left childhood behind.
> You stand on the brink of a journey into the college world,
> or the military.

> Several of you families are preparing to move to new cities
> because of a job change or special family circumstances.

Some of us, of course, may be on the brink of change and don't even
know it.

> How graphically we were reminded of that this week with the tragic
> crash that killed four young people from Ridgefield High School.

> How many lives were altered in that moment!

Because tomorrow is uncertain for all of us, even the young and
strong,
> there are choices that must be faced now,
> MADE NOW!

> Among those choices is the very greatest one.

The choice Joshua held before his people centuries ago.
CHOOSE... WHOM YOU WILL SERVE!

What will control your life? Who will be your GOD?

For that is, without doubt, LIFE'S CHIEF and most URGENT DECISION.

It will have an impact on every other decision –
the mate you select,
the friendships you pursue,
the values you will fight for,
the very words you decide to speak.

Finally, most urgently, it will shape your ETERNAL DESTINY.

WHOM WILL <u>YOU</u> SERVE?

It's not a simple decision.
There are competitors vying for your allegiance.

Joshua mentions three of them.

"You might choose," he says, **the GODS YOUR FATHERS SERVED.**

That's one choice. Imitate your PARENTS.
Adopt their values. Live as they did.

That may be a very good thing.
Or it may not, especially if, as Joshua points out,
your parents have devoted their lives to some empty things –
some IDOLS.

Here is the father who worshipped his WORK –
so much so that it came before his marriage and his kids,
and at the expense of his health.

Here is a mother whose idol was STATUS.

"How do we compare with them?" she always fretted.
   She had to have more things, win more awards.
   Anything but first place was a failure.

Here are the children watching their parents —
   absorbing their prejudices,
      attempting the same frantic schedule,
         learning to handle stress with alcohol,
            speaking the same angry profanities.

If that's how your PARENTS lived, Joshua asks,
will you be content to repeat their mistakes,
   or will you break new ground?

   You're not a kid any more.
      CHOOSE WHOM YOU WILL SERVE!

On the other hand, says Joshua, you might choose
   the GODS OF THE AMORITES IN WHOSE LAND YOU DWELL.

   That's a second option.
      Do what everybody around you does. Conform. Blend in.
         Wear the same clothes.
            Laugh at the same jokes.

   Turn off your BRAIN. Serve their IDOLS.

   What are those?
      Open your eyes, and you'll see soon enough...
      PLAYBOY bunny ears dangle from the rear-view mirrors of
      some of the Amorites among whom we dwell.

      Others carry their portable god down in a six-pack.

      And everywhere we see signs of the 'Almighty' —
      Almighty Dollar, that is!

Advice on how to get rich, including reminders
that you could win $220 million in the latest power-ball
lottery.

MONEY, BOOZE, AND SEX – the unholy trinity in this land of the
Amorites where we dwell.

Will you join the crowd – that technically savvy but spiritually
hungry crowd?
Or stand on your own?

CHOOSE! **CHOOSE WHOM YOU WILL SERVE!**

For everyone finally serves Someone or Something.
Some 'god' or other.

How much better if you choose to serve the god who really <u>is GOD</u>!

Joshua spoke from a solid conviction. He had made his choice.
As for me and my house, we will serve the LORD!

The LORD GOD is no idol, no empty sham.
No figment of someone's imagination.

No indeed! He's the one who IMAGINED <u>US</u>,
and then created us.

He's the one True God, worth loving and serving.
Other things will let you down.
He won't!

So Joshua urges them:
Now therefore, fear the LORD and serve Him!

Though he was speaking to the Israelites, God's own chosen people,
He did not take their choice for granted.
We must not either.

100

Parents, you cannot assume
    your children will choose to serve the Lord
    because they were baptized and brought up in a Christian home.

As a pastor, I dare not assume
    that YOU will make the right choice
    just because you sit attentively here in church right now.

    Or that, once having made that choice,
        you will never change your minds and drift away
        to something else!

    Did you know that 85% of our young people
        drop out of church by age 25?

So it is my job – every preacher's job! - to confront people with
Joshua's challenge...
    CHOOSE! **CHOOSE WHOM YOU WILL SERVE!**

    For it is not only Joshua, nor merely the preacher,
    who is doing the asking.
        God is making His appeal through us.

And here is the Good News.
    He who asks us to choose...HAS ALREADY CHOSEN US!

    In the Bible, the verb 'choose' most often has GOD as the subject.

    He chose Abraham and Sarah to start the nation Israel.
        He chose Moses and Joshua to lead them through the
        Wilderness into Canaan.
            He chose judges, kings, and prophets.

    Over and over, though Israel was stiff-necked and stubborn,
        He chose to stay faithful to them.

    And wonder of wonders, He chooses US – even in the midst of our rebellion, our self-doubt, and our most shameful sins.

You did not choose me, Jesus told the Twelve, **but I chose YOU!**

That girl with the marriage proposal, you see,
has already BEEN CHOSEN!
Already her prospective groom has said,
"I love you. I choose you."

It is hers to accept or reject.

God has already chosen US.
He dispatched His Son into the world to bring that message in
person, saying,
Come, follow me!

For every frightened and unworthy heart,
for every conscience that says,
"I cannot, for my sins are too great,"
He paid the cost of that sin with His blood.

No sin, no bad habit, no past failure has claim on us any more!

Now the risen Jesus stands before us, beckoning us to follow.
But he will not twist our arms.

He waits, while His spokesmen knock on our heart's door and say,
CHOOSE WHOM YOU WILL SERVE!

If the drunkenness, the dishonesty, and the destruction of our families
is to stop
in our homes and classrooms, our neighborhoods,
and in the offices across this land,

if a genuinely new beginning to a life is to be made,
someone will have to trust His gracious call and say,

102

"Yes, Lord, I will follow YOU!"

Back in the 1960s in the midst of the Cold War,
  Billy Graham conducted a crusade in the heart of Russia.

  He preached at a Russian Orthodox church, and at the end of his
  message, he extended the call he always made,
    asking if there were any people listening that night
    who were willing to say yes, to follow the Lord Jesus Christ.

  There was a silence. At the fringe of the crowd, KGB agents
  watched carefully,
    pencils poised over notebooks to write down names.

  Nevertheless, in that crowd, several brave souls raised their hands,
  then came forward.

Today it is your turn.

God's love has reached out in Jesus Christ
and chosen you to serve Him,
  to lead an upright, cheerful, godly life,
    to serve others in His name.

  Will you hear it? Respond to it?

It is a life-changing decision – one that needs making again and again.
  CHOOSE...
    THIS DAY...
      WHOM YOU WILL SERVE!

LOVE'S LOYALTY
The Book of Ruth

_____

My sermon today is about LOVE.

Since that is a topic too large for any sermon,
   I want to narrow it down to one particular facet, namely
      love's LOYALTY -- its FAITHFULNESS.

The inspiration for this message is a woman whose name literally means 'friend'
   and whose life demonstrated what the loyalty of love and friendship are all about.

Her name was RUTH
   and her story is told in the Bible book that bears her name.

READ (with explanatory comments)
1:1-5   1:15-21   4:13-17

Ruth's story teaches us that REAL LOVE aspires to loyalty.
   It is willing to make BIG PROMISES...

   Where you go, I will go...

      Out of love, Ruth is saying, "I am willing to LEAVE everything
      I have known...leave it behind..."
         ALL FOR YOU!

   Your people shall be my people...

      In other words, "I am willing to live in a different country, and
      learn their speech and customs – to stop being a Moabite and
      start being an Israelite..."
         ALL FOR YOU!

Your God shall be my God.

"I hereby renounce my old religion – my old god Chemosh - and embrace a new religion. I will worship Yahweh…"
ALL FOR YOU!

Where you die I will die…

"I make this commitment – not for a month, nor for a year, nor just for 'as long as I can stand it' ….NO, but until I die!"
ALL FOR YOU!

One could hardly make a more comprehensive commitment!

That is why I read these words each time I perform a wedding ceremony.
As the couple kneels at the threshold of a new life, I read these words to urge them to be FAITHFUL – LOYAL to one another.

Who is willing to make such extravagant promises?

The answer is ALL WHO GENUINELY LOVE!

HUSBANDS AND WIVES, who stand at the altar and say with trembling lips,
"Till death do us part."

And not only HUSBANDS AND WIVES,
but other relatives too - parents and children, brothers and sisters.
"You're my flesh and blood. I'll never stop loving you."

Not only RELATIVES,
but FRIENDS TOO make promises of loyalty.
"You can count on me. I won't let you down."

CONFIRMANDS say the same thing here at the Altar:
"God, I love you and I promise to be faithful unto death rather than fall away"

You have made such promises, haven't you?
And others have made them to you.

But love's loyalty is more than TALK.
Real loyalty is proved in ACTION.

Ruth proved her loyalty to Naomi in action.

As the story recounts, she did in fact leave home
and go with Naomi to live in Bethlehem.

She went to work to provide food – sweaty, back-breaking work
called 'gleaning' (picking up leftover grain in harvest fields).

Most amazingly, she willingly entered a marriage with an older man
named Boaz, one of Naomi's relatives, to provide Naomi with
both financial security and an heir … all at Naomi's urging.

This marriage, we should note, was not a romantic match. Boaz
remarks that he's amazed Ruth has not married a younger man.

Has love been so LOYAL in your own experience?

Have you been loyal to your spouse, your relatives, your friends –
and they to you?

Make no mistake, loyalty can be exceedingly hard,
especially if there's a disagreement between you – if one HURTS
the other or BETRAYS the loyalty expected.

Here at CHURCH, as in any other group,
we experience our share of disagreement and conflict.
Promises made on sunny days evaporate when the clouds roll in.

Some of you will remember the disagreement that split our staff a decade ago.

Some will remember the hurts that surfaced over our mission –
The Church of the Master in Canby.
> I wasn't here at the time, but when I arrived I heard plenty
> about it – sometimes from people who had decided
> to leave Trinity.

I also observed a large number of troubled marriages in this congregation,
> more than I had seen in other places I had served.

We know from bitter experience that even among the people of God,
> love is not always loyal.
> It can be and is eroded by unkind words and deeds.

For sooner or later, all of us stumble into sin.
The words of the confession become painfully personal:
> *We have not loved you with our whole heart. We have not
> loved our neighbors as ourselves.*

Just there – when we do wrong, when we fail –
> is when we most need loyal love.

But where shall we find it?

Human love has its limits.

Most of us have a point where we finally say,
> "That's the last straw! You've done it to me once too often.
> I'm through!"

When we say things like that,
> marriages end in divorce,
> > once-close friendships grow distant,
> > > relatives stop visiting or corresponding,

staff members resign,
      congregations divide.

The common human advice about such things is to say,
    "If you want to have a friend, be a friend."

    Yes, that's good advice as far as it goes.
      But what if you are too angry? Too tired?
      What if your hope for lasting love has died?

Then you will need more than GOOD ADVICE!

So what I share with you in this sermon is more than good advice.
    I share GOOD NEWS!

    Good News for all those who are too tired,
                  too angry,
                     too hopeless to be a friend any more.

To you I say,
    You can BE a friend, because you HAVE such a friend.

    One who loves you even though He knows all about you.
    One who has been and will be LOYAL even when you grow OLD,
                 even when you are DISAGREEABLE,
      and especially when you SIN!

Such a friend we have in JESUS...all those sins and griefs to bear.

This Jesus made BIG PROMISES to you.

    "Where you go I will go."
      YES, **I am with you always, to the end of the age.**

    "Where you die I will die."
      YES, **The Good Shepherd lays down his life for the sheep.**

Jesus kept his promises to you.
He laid down His life for you,
and He has been with you through all kinds of trials, has he not?

Trips to the emergency room and the employment office,
to municipal court and the funeral home.

Two years ago we held a service on the first anniversary of
the terrorist attacks on September 11.

I still remember one of our couples who stood in front of us during
that service describing the faithful love of God that sustained
them through twin family disasters -
the husband losing his job at United Airlines
and the wife being diagnosed with cancer
at nearly the same time.

Have you ever stood as they did, looking back over some dark night
of the soul, saying, "How did we ever make it?"
and realizing with sudden clarity that it is no mystery,
that it is He, our Savior and Lord,
who has been carrying us all along?

What a Friend we have in Jesus, all our sins and griefs to bear!

And because we <u>have</u> such a loyal friend, we can <u>be</u> loyal to others.
WE LOVE…BECAUSE HE FIRST LOVED US!

He didn't wait for us to seek or to beg.
He came before we sought Him,
Yes, even as we hated Him, resented Him, rebelled against Him!

He made the first move. And He keeps on coming to us,
even when we flinch and falter and fail.

The cross was history's clearest demonstration of the loyal,
long-suffering love of God.

110

His love has made all the difference for US.

When we receive it, and then share it,
    such loyal love makes a big difference to OTHERS.

Ruth's loyalty changed everything for Naomi.

At the start of the book, Naomi returns to Bethlehem with an embittered spirit:
    Call me Marah, she says, **for the Lord has dealt very bitterly with me.**

But at the end of the book, Naomi is holding Ruth's baby Obed in her arms and her neighbors are laughing joyfully with her:
    Blessed be the Lord, who has not left you this day without kin!

Loyalty does that.
    It turns bitter people into blessed people, so that they give God a hallelujah.

But there is more.
    Love and Loyalty are a blessing not only to those who RECEIVE, but to those who GIVE as well.

Little did Ruth expect, as she set out for Bethlehem,
that she would soon set foot in the village
    where her Savior Jesus was to be born...

Even less did she suspect that SHE would be included in His family tree!

That's how God surprises those who bear life's burdens,
    and remain loyal to Him and to each other.

Maybe you are saying to yourself,
    "It's too late for me. The damage is done.
    The relationship is destroyed.

It is too late for love or loyalty to do any good."

If you think so, listen to this true story.
Two young men were growing up together around the turn of the last century.
As neighbors they had played together, gone to school together, been on the same teams, and become fast friends.

When the First World War erupted, they enlisted together in the Army.
By chance they were put into the same unit
and found themselves on the same battlefield.

After one particularly bitter day of fighting, one of the young men was discovered to be missing.

The other boy, safe and unhurt, asked his commanding officer for permission to go out into 'no man's land' and look for his friend.
"It's no use," he was told. "Nothing could be alive out there after the withering fire of so many hours."

But he persisted, and his commander reluctantly agreed.
Sometime later he returned, bearing the lifeless body of his friend over his shoulder.
The commander said sadly, "Didn't I tell you it was no use?"

"Oh, but it was," said the boy.
"I got there in time to hear him whisper, 'I KNEW YOU'D COME!'"

As long as life remains, it isn't too late to share the love you have received from God.

There is someone, isn't there, who needs it from you?
Maybe your husband or wife.
Maybe your alienated friend or neighbor.
Maybe a person who months or years ago left this church.

It may be that this other person did something to hurt you.
   Maybe you were the 'innocent party.'

No matter!

Love's loyalty will go the extra mile.
   It will shoulder more than its share of the blame.
   It will do whatever it can to seek and find the other and deliver a
      loving word.

That's what Jesus did, and still does, for you this very day.
   That's who is waiting to meet you in those encounters we
   sometimes dread.

So go.
   When you meet that person, in that same moment,
   you will meet your Savior too...
      and He will whisper, "I knew you'd come."

GOD SENT NATHAN
2 Samuel 12:1-15

Every year the motion picture industry presents Oscars.

There are Oscars for Best Picture, Best Director, Best Actor and Actress, and so on.

One that interests me especially is for 'Best Supporting Actor.'
    A supporting actor has a lesser role,
       but he's still important, because he can highlight the main character and even improve his performance.

A Bible story that has inspired at least one movie
is the story of King David.
    It features a complex plot line,
          lots of action,
             and memorable characters.

If Oscars were to be given out to the characters in this story,
    David himself would be the 'Best Actor.'

But there's another character whose role fascinates me,
about whom I'd like to preach to you today -
    a man who, though he appears seldom in the story, plays a crucial role.

    He helped David make a mid-course correction,
       and possibly saved him eternally.

For 'Best Supporting Actor,' I nominate Nathan, the prophet.

Nathan makes three appearances in David's story.
    The FIRST is when David is contemplating building the TEMPLE.

"NO!" said Nathan. "You are not the one to build it."
He then went on to reveal God's astonishing promise that David's dynasty will last forever.

The THIRD is when David is dying,
and a successor must be chosen from among his many sons.

Nathan helped persuade David to select Solomon – and David heeded the prophet's advice.

But the SECOND appearance is the most memorable of the three.
It is the most urgent, and the most dangerous for Nathan, for he literally took his life in his hands that day.

The story unfolds in 2 Samuel.

David has stumbled into horrible wickedness.

He has seen a beautiful woman bathing on a rooftop.
She is Bathsheba, the wife of one of his army captains.
He has seduced her, gotten her pregnant,
and then murdered her husband to cover it up.

He pretends to be the kindly benefactor who has taken this grieving widow under his wing to care for her in her time of distress!

Whereupon God dispatches Nathan to confront the King and rebuke him.

READ THE TEXT

What an assignment for Nathan!

Go unbidden to stand before the king.
Tell him his sins.
Call him an adulterer and a murderer who has despised God.

116

Then announce the punishment – including the death of the child!

Can you imagine how Nathan must have felt?

Maybe like the GIs headed for the deadly beaches of Normandy, and all the waiting German guns…
or like the trembling Christians dispatched to meet hungry lions in the Coliseum!

But Nathan does not balk.

He goes.
He takes his life in his hands.
He stands before the King, that lion of a man, points a trembling finger, and speaks the judgment of God:
YOU ARE THE MAN!

I nominate Nathan, first, because of his COURAGE!

But he has another quality too –
one that enabled David to listen to his
terrible words, take them to heart, and finally confess his sin.

Nathan has WISDOM.

He chooses his words carefully.
Frames them in such a way that the truth
can be inserted into David's heart before David realized it.

My dentist used a similar tactic with me.
I had told him that I had a low threshold for pain –
that I feared the needle.

So he adopted a sneaky tactic.
He had me close my eyes, whereupon he grasped my lip and gave it a shake.

I did not notice until afterward that he had deftly inserted
the needle into my gum while I was distracted!

Nathan does that to David.

He grabs hold of his attention with a pathetic story
about a rich man who took and butchered a poor man's
lamb.

David's attention is focused on that heartless man.
His anger rises.
He pronounces JUDGMENT!

Only when the story was finished and the sentence pronounced
does David realize
that Nathan has inserted the needle
into his own heart....
YOU ARE THE MAN!

God's Word and Nathan's wisdom leads to an astonishing result.

The king bows his head and quietly confesses:
I have sinned against the Lord.

David is broken. His spirit humbled.
And now Nathan speaks his most important line:
The Lord has put away your sin.

In that moment the AGENT OF JUDGMENT
becomes the SPOKESMAN OF GOD'S GRACE.

The name Nathan means 'Gift.'

Nathan is God's GIFT to David,
bringing the two words a sinner needs most to hear:

The Word of LAW to bring him to repentance and

the Word of GRACE to comfort and forgive.

Every sinner needs a NATHAN!
    You do. So do I. For we are no better than David.

If our sins are not as spectacular, they are no less deadly.

Like David, we cover them up
    so that no one would guess by looking what has gone wrong in
    our lives.

But God knows, so He sends a Nathan to us.

WHO IS THE NATHAN IN YOUR LIFE?

Is it the pastor… who preaches a sermon that, as some say,
"hit me between the eyes"
    or calls us on the phone at an eerily coincidental moment?

Perhaps the Nathan is someone even closer:
    a co-worker
        who corners us in the parking lot and asks,
        "What's up with you these days?"
    or a spouse
        who finally erupts in anger or tears,
        pleading for us to change our ways…
    or a child
        who looks at us with wide eyes, begging for our attention.

And if we will not listen to any of those people, God may send a
'printed Nathan' -
    a passage of Scripture that arrests us
    or a reading from a book or pamphlet that gives us a lump in the
        throat and needles us about our sin.

How do you react to the Nathans who come to you?
    Do you resent the pastor's inquiry, saying

119

"Why do you keep pestering me? I don't like to be pushed!"

Do you brush aside your spouse?
  "Quit your nagging!"

Ignore your child?

Change the subject with your co-worker?

Or will you do as David did - bow your head,
                    leave the excuses behind,
            and make a simple confession:
    I have sinned against the Lord?

"Nathan means 'GIFT.'

Shall we not accept the NATHANS God sends as gifts of mercy
    to bring us to our senses before it is too late
    so that we can open our hearts to hear the pardoning word
    The Lord has put away your sin!

For He HAS!
    Jesus paid your debt.
    Bled and died for you.
    Lifted that heavy burden you've tried to carry by yourself.
    Entered your death, your grave, and came out again alive!

    In the book *Pilgrim's Progress* is a scene in which Pilgrim,
        struggling along with a heavy bundle of sins on his back,
        comes to the mouth of Christ's empty tomb.

    The bundle suddenly slides from his shoulders and rolls into
    the tomb, never to be seen again!

    Come unto me, says Jesus, **all you who labor and are heavy-
    laden, and I will give you REST!**

Thank God for the Nathans who tell us that comforting word,
who show us Jesus, the crucified and Risen One, the Burden-lifter!

Now let me turn it completely around: COULD YOU BE A NATHAN?

Every sinner needs one.
That includes your spouse, your child,
your teammates, your boss
and yes, your PASTOR too!

Each one of these people sins,
and each finally needs some word from God to bring him to
repentance so that he may find peace.

If not you, WHO? If not now, WHEN?

It happened to me one evening. I phoned a woman who had been
missing from church for a long time. I was thinking of myself as her
Nathan.

In the midst of our talk, she plucked up courage and said to me,
"Pastor, I have a hard time coming back because you intimidate
me by your confrontive manner."

Though it was fearful for her, she dared to be a Nathan to me,
and through her God taught me that I needed to be gentler,
more compassionate.

It's hard to be a Nathan!
It requires courage. And a generous helping of WISDOM.
It means that we must speak honestly about uncomfortable things.

But in the end, it allows us to speak helpfully of Jesus Christ
and His grace to one another.

That's the best supporting action you can give. King David would tell
you that.

MAKE A WISH!
1 Kings 3:5-12

"Make a wish!"
    You're poised in front of a birthday cake.
    The candles are lit and everyone is waiting and watching.

    Someone has a camera pointed at you, ready to capture the
    moment.
       "Go on, make a wish!"

So do you?
    Or do you simply dispense with the wishing
    and huff and puff your candles out?

Children don't seem to have any trouble making wishes.
    Whether in front of a birthday cake
    or sitting on Santa's lap at Macy's,
       they can always think of something to wish for.

And we encourage them!
    We read them stories about Pinocchio wishing on a star to become
    a real boy
       or Snow White wishing her prince would come.

We adults, it would appear, don't do as much wishing,
    and when we do, our wishes are of a different sort.

    We make wishes for our kids and grandkids
    or what we'll do when we retire.

Perhaps some of you will think it silly to talk about making wishes here
in church.
    This is a place where we talk about sin and forgiveness,
    about obedience and love and 'spiritual things.'

True enough! But the Bible also has a lot to say about WISHING,
   and in fact encourages us to do it.

   There's nothing silly about what Jesus said:
      Ask, and it shall be given you.

   Some of the Bible's best stories
      tell of people who dared to wish for great things
      and saw those wishes come true!

One of those stories is about Solomon.

Listen to the words of 1 Kings 3:

READ THE TEXT

There's a lot to learn in this story.
   The very first lesson is: MAKE A WISH!

   That's what God is saying to Solomon in his dream that night:
      ASK FOR WHATEVER YOU WANT ME TO GIVE YOU!

Someone might object by saying,
   "This is not about wishing. This is about PRAYING!"

   Well, what's the difference between wishing and praying?
      Isn't it simply that a PRAYER is a wish directed to the right place,
      to a listening, caring God?

   Put another way, a PRAYER is a wish with teeth in it!

Notice that GOD takes the initiative.
   It is not like Aladdin's Lamp, where it's all up to Aladdin – where
   Aladdin must find the lamp,
      rub it the right way,
         and summon the genie.

124

No, in Scripture it is the other way around.
 God takes the initiative! Here in this story, God comes
 unbidden to Solomon, calls out, and invites him to make a wish.

Ask what I shall give you God says to Solomon.

Ask and it shall be given you says Jesus to us.

So do we?

I have met many gloomy people who have given up wishing for
anything at all.
 They expect life to disappoint them, and it does.
 They aim at nothing – and hit it!

The Apostle James says something startling in his letter:
 You do not have because you do not ask.

We must admit that life carries a goodly share of heartache and
disappointment.
 But at least some of that is because
 WE NEVER THOUGHT TO PRAY ABOUT THINGS IN THE FIRST PLACE!

Years ago when I began serving a congregation in Ohio,
 I decided that in my first round of visits to people,
 I would ask each person the same thing:
  "If God appeared to you in a dream tonight and said,
  'I will give you whatever you wish for about your church,'
  what would you wish for?"

A surprising number of the people could think of nothing at all –
 nothing to ask God for.

Maybe that's YOU.

Maybe you are unhappy with life
 disappointed in your family,

bored with your job,
  feeling unimportant, unappreciated,
    or just plain tired of it all.

If so, won't you hear God's call to you in this story?

MAKE A WISH!
  Bring it to Him, who is able, says Ephesians 3,
    to do far more than all we ask or even think!

Look further at this story. Hear Solomon's stunning response:
  **O Lord, my God...I am only a little child and do not know how
  to carry out my duties... give me a discerning heart to govern
  your people and to distinguish right from wrong...**

If God's invitation is the first lesson - MAKE A WISH –
  then Solomon's response is the second lesson:
    MAKE IT A <u>GOOD</u> WISH!

Remember that Solomon was a very young man when this story took
place, probably in his early twenties.

  Think about what the typical 20-year-old American male might ask
  if given such a blank check by God -
    a fast car
      a hot lady
        a six-pack of Budweiser
          and lots of spending money,
            if we are to believe the Madison Avenue pitchmen.

But there's nothing typical about Solomon.
  His request is astonishingly different, so much so that even God
  appears surprised:
    "You asked for this, and not for long life? Or wealth for
    yourself? Or the death of your enemies?"

126

No. Solomon had fixed his mind elsewhere – on something very good: **Give your servant a discerning heart.**

Instead of asking for THINGS,
Solomon asks that he might become a different PERSON.

A 'discerning heart' means, literally, a 'hearing heart.'

Solomon wants a deep inner connection with God –
    so that in his 'heart of hearts' he would always hear God's voice
    and thus know the difference between wise and foolish, right
    and wrong.

All of which prompts me to ask, WHAT ABOUT OUR PRAYERS?
    What is it we are asking God for?

Too often, one writer observed, our prayers are a barometer –
not of our HOLINESS, but of our WICKEDNESS.

The MATERIALISTIC person
    asks God for more and more things – a second home,
                           a larger boat,
                              the latest electronic devices,
                  a stock market always on the rise.

The VENGEFUL person
    may pray that God will 'teach so-and-so a lesson' and straighten
    him out, preferably by sending him some suffering or loss.

Our prayers may reveal just how godless we are!

I met a woman years ago who told me that she was praying
for a certain man to become her husband.

She had to pray for it, she explained, because he was still married
to someone else!

The Apostle James says about such prayers,
You ask, but do not receive, because you ask wrongly,
to spend it on your passions.

Take a lesson from Solomon.
MAKE YOUR WISH A GOOD WISH — a godly one,
and most of all that you might come closer to God and what He
wants for you.

It can happen, you know!
This story teaches that we are not bringing our wishes to a magic
lamp, or a wishing star, or a leprechaun,
but to the Almighty and Wise God Himself,
who has promised to hear and answer us.

That is the third lesson in this story, the best lesson of all:
WE HAVE A GOD WHO GRANTS GOOD WISHES.

We sang it in the hymn a few minutes ago:
You are coming to a king
Large petitions with you bring
For His grace and power are such
None can ever ask too much!

God granted Solomon's wish in short order.

Solomon became a new, a different man, renowned for his wisdom.
A few verses later in this chapter, two women came before him,
each claiming the same baby as her own.
Calmly, coolly, Solomon ordered his attendant
to take a sword and divide the child, giving half to each
woman.

Amid the gasps of observers, his wisdom proved true, for the
real mother cried out in anguish,
"Give him to her, but spare his life!"

128

Thereby he identified the true mother
and ordered the baby given to her.

Solomon's wisdom became legendary,
and people came from all over the world just to listen to him.

Three books in the Bible are attributed to him – a testimony to
how powerfully God answered his good wish.

It was even better than that, for God did more than what He
promised, as He so often does!
I will give you what you have not asked, God told Solomon,
**both riches and honor, so that in all your lifetime you will
have no equal.**

And that happened too.
So wealthy did Solomon become, that, as the Bible narrates,
he made silver as common in Jerusalem as stones.

God did good things for Solomon.
He wants to do good things for you because He loves you!

God has a wish too.
A GOOD wish. A GREAT wish!

His surpassing desire is to take us – people dead in our sins –
and bring us back to life.

What's more He took steps to make sure that His GREAT WISH might
come true. He kept Solomon's descendants on the throne for
hundreds of years,
and from Solomon's line a brought forth a little child who, says
the Bible,
grew in wisdom and stature, and in favor with God and man.

That boy Jesus had a hearing heart too,
a heart that heard the cries of us poor sinners

and came to seek and to save us,
  a heart that heard the Father's directive to
  lay down His life for us.

That Savior made Himself poor,
  that we might become incredibly rich,
  beyond the wealth of Solomon,
    for He has given us treasure in heaven, a life that will never
    end!

That Savior has become our Lord – our Wisdom, our Joy,
  the beating heart of our Life in God.

  Because He's risen from the dead, He has come to take up
  residence in us.
    He 'abides in us' that we may stay close to Him.

  The astonishing result?
    Paul said, **It is no longer I who live, but
    Christ who lives in me!**

    His heart, His wisdom, His love are alive in us
      and all the baptized, in all who trust in Him.

What will you do with such a gift?

Here's a thought.
  If God has given you a 'hearing heart' that is open to him and
  others, then listen to the wants and needs of people around you.

  There is an organization called the Make a Wish Foundation.
    Its goal is to grant the wishes of terminally ill children
    and so brighten their short lives –
      by taking them to meet a sports hero
      or have a wondrous trip to Disney World.

Isn't that what God's church might be in a way?

130

A community of people who listen to the heart cries around us
and bring the power and love of God to bear –
to grant people's desperate wishes for pardon and for peace
and for a life that will last beyond death.

The wish for the church to be all God meant us to be
is a VERY GOOD WISH, don't you think?

May we be wishing that,
and may God in His mercy make it come true
through Jesus Christ our Lord.

THE FROG IN THE KETTLE
1 Kings 11:1-13

It happened one day in a high school biology class - a scene both fascinating and horrible.
The students watched the slow death of a frog
as part of an unforgettable experiment.

The teacher began with a healthy frog in an oversized beaker of cool water.

Beneath the beaker,
he moved a Bunsen burner with a very low flame
so that the water heated slowly, very slowly (.017 F per second).

The temperature rose so gradually that the frog was unaware of the change.

Frogs, the teacher explained, are cold-blooded.
Their body temperature varies to match their environment.

As the water warmed, so did the frog.
Just two hours later the frog was dead – boiled to death.

The change occurred so slowly
That the cold-blooded frog neither tried to jump out
nor unleash a complaining kick!

What happened to that frog
is something that happens to many people.

It may be happening to some of YOU!

The first eleven chapters of 1 Kings record the slow death of a great man – in fact, the greatest man of his day.

That man was Solomon.
The one who made a great prayer-wish for wisdom.
The one whom God answered by granting the prayer and making
him the wisest man who ever lived.

Like that frog, Solomon started healthy, but ended spiritually dead.

Charles Swindoll called Solomon in the end a "debauched,
effeminate cynic,"
an idolater who left his nation confused and conflicted,
and soon to be fractured by a civil war.

Solomon's END is described in 1 Kings 11:

READ THE TEXT

There are at least three cautions in this cautionary tale.

First, EVEN THE GREAT MAY FALL.

Solomon began as a great man.
He was of royal blood.
Blessed with a first-class intellect.
Tutored at the feet of the prophet Nathan,
with his father David as a model for kingship
before his very eyes.
Best of all, say the Scriptures, he loved the Lord.

Solomon HAD IT ALL!
To see him end as he did is chilling.
A reminder of just how weak and frail is our sinful flesh —
even in the best of us.

St. Paul said it plainly:
I know that in me, that is in my flesh, dwells no good thing.

The daily news portrays day after day how the great fall.

134

Catholic priests abusing children.
    Presidents having illicit affairs – right in the White House!
       Sports heroes, idolized by fans, discovered to be
       cheats and liars.

In 1919 there was a baseball player for the Chicago White Sox named 'Shoeless' Joe Jackson. He was highly regarded, but the fans didn't know that Joe Jackson and others had conspired to throw the World Series for money.

When the story finally broke, many still couldn't believe it. As Jackson was leaving a meeting one day, a young boy called after him,
       "Say it ain't so, Joe!"

Ah, but it WAS so, and it IS so with many a good and decent man and woman
    seduced by the Devil, the world, or their own sinful flesh.

It happens with regularity in the church, not because the church is especially corrupt, but because
       THAT'S HOW PEOPLE ARE!

It has happened in every church I have served, to all manner of people, and most shockingly to the leaders, people I respected.
    A congregation president who abandoned his family and broke up a friend's marriage.
       An elder's wife who embezzled $40,000 from her company.
       A retired pastor who drifted into alcoholism and quit the church.

Here's the scariest part:
    It could happen to anyone, including you!

That's the first caution. Now comes a second.
SUCH PERSONAL DESTRUCTION IS ALMOST ALWAYS GRADUAL.

No garden 'suddenly' overgrows with weeds.
No congregation 'suddenly' splits.
No building 'suddenly' crumbles.
No marriage 'suddenly' breaks apart.

The changes that come into our lives and take hold and finally destroy us happen slowly,
like the heating of the water
in that beaker in biology class.

Slowly, imperceptibly, things that once shocked us
no longer do.
We come to accept behaviors we formerly condemned,
and we explain it by saying we have 'matured.'

Things once identified as harmful
are first tolerated, then sampled, and finally accepted and defended.

In his book on marriage entitled *AS FOR ME AND MY HOUSE*, author Walt Wangerin includes a chapter on avoiding adultery. He writes:

Adultery is never a sudden, spontaneous, and totally unexpected act. It is always preceded by a longer drama, at the beginning of which you are not helpless... early on in an extramarital friendship there comes a moment of 'maybe'... You may sense the feeling of further possibility... whether it ends here, or continues hereafter, a door has opened... If you do not say NO, you have, by your silence, approved the maybe... Let no one say of his adultery, 'I couldn't help it.' For there was a moment when he could have closed the door.

The surest road to hell is the gradual one, for there is nothing startling to waken us or rouse us to turn back.

Say it this way: SIN MAKES US COLD-BLOODED.

It coaxes us to adapt to the temperature of the culture around us, to conform, to compromise
  so that we cannot see the deadliness of the changes we experience.

Like the frog in the kettle, Solomon began slowly boiling to death,
  but he seemed unaware of it.

  Are you, am I, fully aware of the changes happening
  in our values and our behaviors?

  Are we willing to stop now? To say NO?

There is a third caution in this story.
  AN EVIL END OFTEN BEGINS
  WITH SOMETHING THAT SOUNDS AND FEELS GOOD.

  King Solomon, the story says, **loved many...women.**
  Later it adds that he **held fast to them in love.**

  Is there any sweeter word in our language than 'love'?
  Can there be anything finer than to 'fall in love' or to 'be in love'?

  Love is a good word. It's a Bible word!

  It can't be wrong when it feels so right,
    sang Debby Boone in a pop song a few years back.

  So Solomon loved women, modern folks would say. That's healthy.
  That's manly.

But not all loves are the same. And not all are healthy!
  An alcoholic loves his booze, and that love will be the death of him.
    A glutton loves to eat, but that eating may destroy his health.
      An adulterer loves another person – but she is
      the wrong person,
        and this illicit 'love' may finally ruin his family.

Some loves God forbids!
Jesus said, **He who loves father or mother more than me
is not worthy of me.**

Any love that comes before the love of God
or leads us to disobey God
is a love forbidden.

Solomon's loves were forbidden loves.
God had forbidden marriage to 'foreign women,' those who
worshipped other gods,
for He knew they would lead their husbands into idolatry.

It happened with Solomon.
His wives, says the holy writer, **led him astray...** they
turned his heart after other gods.

Some of the loves that control us are deceitful and deadly.

"I'm only doing this because I love you," says a domineering parent,
whose brand of love has begun to squeeze the life out of the child.

"I just love having a good time," says the college student,
explaining why she has been drinking to excess.

So it is that when Luther explains the first commandment in his
Small Catechism he writes,
We are to fear, love, and trust in God above all things.

Do we?

Beware, friend!
Let this cautionary tale teach you that not all loves are lovely,
that some may be deadly.

That brings us to a fourth and final point in this cautionary tale,
a point that is not a caution, but an encouragement!

There is another love at work in this story: THE LOVE OF GOD.
   A love that was at work before Solomon was born.
      A love that continued to work after Solomon died.

The love of God was what set the story in motion long before.
   It was a love that called Israel out of Egypt,
   and brought them into this land.
      It was a love that had put Solomon's father David on the
      throne and made a promise to stay faithful to David's line
      forever.

Even in His anger at Solomon's sin, God remembered His love for
David.
   After pronouncing punishment for Solomon,
   God tempers His judgment with mercy:
      Nevertheless, for the sake of David your father,
      I will not do it during your lifetime.

We are not told if Solomon repented.
   We don't know if he remained unwilling to change.

But we do know what came afterward.

   God's love for David stayed constant.
   He finally sent His own Son to become a Son of David
      to save all those who had gotten into hot water!

Jesus wasn't cold-blooded. He was warm-blooded.

   A warm-blooded creature
      Is one whose body maintains a constant temperature
      in spite of its surroundings.

Jesus' love didn't vary with the latest polls. It stayed constant.
   It wasn't deterred by our fickleness or His own pain.
   It stayed true to the Father's plan to save us.

He shed His warm blood on the cross,
and that warm-blooded love makes a difference
to people who hear of it and trust in Him.

The love of Christ controls us wrote Saint Paul.

God's love takes people who have made a bad beginning
and brings them to a good end.
It brings hope to those of us who, like Solomon, have drifted
into something deadly.

There's no hope for the frog.

But there IS hope for you and me.
God tempered His judgment on Solomon **for the sake of David.**
To us He is merciful **for the sake of Jesus.**

Aren't you glad?

Still, it is good to hear the story of Solomon, a cautionary tale
both sad and sobering.

The memory of Solomon's end may help to keep us
out of hot water!

LEASE ON A NEW LIFE
2 Kings 20:1-7

(Funeral Sermon for Ron Baker)

Back in the cold days of February,
we observed a special moment here at church.
    It was Ron's fiftieth birthday celebration, and a happy day it was,
        made all the sweeter by the realization of the extra years of life
        he had been given.

    I remember that day, and Ron's shy smile.

What a story is Ron Baker's life!
    Every life, of course, is a story worth hearing.
    Every life has something to teach us if we will listen to it, ponder it.

    And when the person is a believer, as Ron was,
      we behold the added dimension of the mysterious, gracious
      working of God.

But Ron's story went far beyond the ordinary.
    He said it himself: "My life is a miracle!"

    For those who may not know it well, I will tell you the miracle story
    once more.

      In the year 1991, Ron was a young, gifted man with life before
      him. Husband. Father of 3 children. Much on his agenda.
        Then, at age 32, a dreadful diagnosis –
        BRAIN CANCER, almost certainly terminal!

    The doctors made a radical proposal:
      the removal of part of the left temporal lobe of his brain, along
      with radiation and chemotherapy.

141

The surgery and the treatments were undertaken,
with an astonishing result:
    Ron's cancer went into remission,
    and he was given a new lease on life -- 18 extra years!

This, as you must know, is a very rare occurrence. Miraculous, even!
    In 37 years of ministry, I had never encountered such a happening.
    It was a story almost Scriptural in its drama.

    There is, in fact, a Bible story very like it, back in the Book of 2
    Kings. Let me read it to you...

READ THE TEXT

The similarities in the stories of these two men are striking.

    Both were young men in their 30s – Hezekiah age 37, Ron age 32.
    Both were believers who had trusted in God.
    Both were diagnosed as 'terminal' –
        Hezekiah by the prophet Isaiah,
        Ron by the doctor.

    And both received a NEW LEASE ON LIFE –
        Hezekiah for 15 years, Ron for 18.

    Both filled their years with useful service to God and others.

I said at the start of this message
    that every life has something to teach us if we will listen to it and
    ponder it.

    What is it, do you suppose, God would have us learn
        as we consider these two men?

I will start with something simple, but deeply important.
    We need to learn that
    our LIVES, AND ALL OUR YEARS, ARE A GIFT FROM GOD.

142

Whether long or short, or somewhere in between,
   LIFE IS A GIFT!

We say that... but we don't usually mean it.

In fact, most of us feel that we are entitled to a long, happy life.
We expect 80 years or more!
   God owes it to us.

   When someone dies young, or encounters heartache,
   we say they've been 'cheated.'

So we go about our business,
      presuming on our good health, our happiness,
      and our prosperity,

         often not appreciating the preciousness of the gift,
         until something comes along that makes us realize
            how fragile we are,
            and how easily life could end.

Country singer Tim McGraw has a song about that called
LIVE LIKE YOU WERE DYING. In it two men are talking,
and one says,
   I was in my early 40s, with a lot of life before me
   When a moment came that stopped me on a dime
   I spent most of the next days lookin' at the x-rays
   And talkin' about the options,
   And talkin' about sweet time

      I asked him when it sank in,
      That this might really be the real end,
      "How's it hitcha when you get that kind of news?"

If you asked King Hezekiah, or Ron, or any of the people who've gotten
   "that kind of news," you will hear them testify in no uncertain
   terms,

NOW I KNOW THAT LIFE IS A GIFT!

Often there are tears.
Hezekiah wept, and Ron did his share too!
So have some of you...

LIFE IS A GIFT! That's the first lesson.

A second lesson follows on the first:
THAT GIFT, THAT LIFE, IS MEANT TO BE FILLED, NOT WASTED!

King Hezekiah made the most of his 'new lease on life.'

In those 15 years, he undertook a project that became the great
accomplishment of his reign:
Hezekiah directed his men to dig a tunnel
from the Gihon Spring outside Jerusalem's walls
back to the city.
They added a reservoir for the re-directed water.
Finally he had his workmen permanently cover the
spring so that the only access was through the tunnel.

All of this to protect the city during any siege laid against it.

The city enjoyed greater safety because Hezekiah used his
'new lease on life.'

Ron knew that his years, too, were a gift, and he intended to make
the most of them.
At church he made himself available to help wherever he could.
At home, he was a man on a mission.
"I want to see my kids grow up!" he said.

And so he did!

He threw his energy into helping each of you, and all were
blessed.

144

I suppose the most dramatic of all the help he gave
was what he did for you, Kris,
    when you experienced that sudden paralysis 7 years ago.

    He willingly took on the role of Mr. Mom and chief caregiver.
    Lots of new things to learn.
      Lots of work.
        Lots of blessing!

    All of you children, and other folks too, were blessed because
    Ron used his
      'new lease on life.'

How about you, my friend, as you ponder this man and his life?
    What have you determined to do with your life? Your years?

Are you KILLING TIME, or FILLING IT with celebration and service?

The man in the song decides to make the most of his days:
    I went sky diving, I went Rocky Mountain climbing,
    I went two point seven seconds on a bull named Fumanchu.
      And I loved deeper and I spoke sweeter
      and I gave forgiveness that I'd been denying.
    I was finally the husband that most of the time I wasn't.

    And I became a friend
      a friend would like to have.
    And all of a sudden going fishin'
      wasn't such an imposition
    And I went three times the year I lost my dad.
    Well, I finally read the Good Book
    And I took a good long hard look
    At what I'd do if I could do it all again...

Today's the day to do that kind of thing, you know...
    to 'take a good long hard look' at what we'd do
    'if we could do it all again.'

To take a look at our relationships.
And not to forget the relationship with God,
  who gave us all these gifts in the first place.

That is the third lesson, one that Ron can teach us especially well:
  CHERISH YOUR RELATIONSHIP WITH LIFE'S GIVER!

  Ron knew not only that life is a gift...
  he knew the Giver and trusted Him.

Long before Ron got a new lease on life in 1991,
  he got a lease on a NEW LIFE, thanks to the grace of His Savior.

  It's what Jesus meant when He said:
    **I am come that they might have life, and have it
    more abundantly!**

  That lease on a new life was made when Ron was a baby.

    Do you remember that day, mom and dad, when Ron was
    baptized at the base chapel in Germany?

    There began a connection with Jesus Christ that lasted through
    all these fifty wonderful years.

A lease on a NEW LIFE!

Ron's NEW LIFE was of a modest length, but it had an extraordinary
DEPTH!
  He enjoyed the fellowship of the church.
  He enjoyed the music played and sung.

  He enjoyed the sweet story of the Savior's love
    read in the Good Book and listened to in church:
      Christmas and the manger,
        the Sermon on the Mount,
          the cross on Calvary,

the empty tomb at Easter.

Ron rejoiced in that story!

Most of all he rejoiced that He was a recipient of that love
that forgave all his sins
    and promised him with absolute certainly that death could not
    cancel the GIFT OF LIFE
        he had by faith in Jesus Christ.

The blessings of such a life spill over far beyond the family circle.
    It was my privilege to overhear your tender words, Hans,
    spoken to Ron the day he died,
        words of appreciation for the example of a life lived
        with integrity and faith.

But I need also to address a difficult truth.
    Any life, even that NEW LIFE GOD GIVES IN JESUS, will face times of
    pain and sorrow.

    The gift of life comes under tremendous pressures.

    God knits us together in families and congregations,
        but there are forces at work that can tear at our hearts
        and make things unravel.

You're facing such a time today.
    It's not the first time your family has faced
    wrenching trials! It surely won't be the last.

    How will we manage? Who will do the things Ron did?
    How can we fill the empty place he leaves?
    How can we keep from unraveling?

Accordingly I ask you to look at one more thing.

Ron's NEW LIFE was hemmed all around by prayer.

His faith knew that life must
be held together that way, lest it come unraveled.
So he would say, "Pray for Kris! Pray for mom!"
"Pray!" he urged us.

St. Paul said the same: **Pray for us, brethren! Pray without ceasing!**

Let us commit to doing that in the days ahead.
You, Jan, Kris, Nicole, and Ben, know how much it meant to dad.
Therefore I urge you to hold one another before God as you pray.

I urge the rest of you to do the same.

Let us all commit to praying for this family,
and for all those God has placed into our lives and hearts.

The same Lord Jesus that loved Ron and listened to Him
loves and listens to you.

Bring Him your burdens today.
Your need for direction and your prayer for joy to be restored.

For the JOY is coming. The JOY Ron knows even better
now that the pain is ended and the eternal life begun.

God grant you a lease on that NEW LIFE, as He did for Ron.

FOR SUCH A TIME AS THIS
Esther 4

_____

One of the neglected books in the Bible is the Book of ESTHER.

Not everyone neglects it, mind you.
The Jewish people love this book
and read it faithfully each year at their festival of Purim.

And once every few years our Sunday school teachers
tell their students the story of brave Queen Esther
saving her people from Haman's plot.

No, it's we PREACHERS who have neglected this book.
In all my life, I have never heard a sermon from the Book of Esther.

Have you?

This morning I want to make amends.
For the story of Esther is not merely good drama.
It has striking relevance for anyone needing courage
in the face of evil...

I'd like to read from Esther chapter 4. But first let's set the stage.

The SETTING is in Persia (modern Iran) in the 5th century BC.
There are many Jewish exiles living there, far from home.

By a strange twist of circumstances, a Jewish girl named Esther has
been chosen as queen by King Ahasuerus,
known to history as Xerxes I.

It is not long before trouble brews.
Haman, a high government official, is angered when
Esther's Uncle Mordecai refuses to bow and honor him.

When Haman learns that Mordecai is a Jew,
  he manipulates the king into making a law allowing the
  killing of all Jews on an appointed day.

As chapter 4 begins, Mordecai has just learned of Haman's plot.
READ 4:1-3

Mordecai alerts Esther.
He instructs her to go to the King and plead for mercy
  for the Jews.

The story resumes...
READ 4:11-16

Why should we pay attention to this story?

First, because it tells us about a CRUCIAL MOMENT in history.
  A time of crisis – of urgent danger.

The Jews in Persia are faced with genocide at the hand of a
madman.

Does that sound familiar?
  That this is no mere Sunday School story ought to be clear to us
  who remember that just 70 years ago,
    a madman named Adolf Hitler
    put to death some 6 million Jews in Europe.

Who knows, says Mordecai to Esther, **whether you have not come to
the kingdom for such a time as this?**

No time is free from such moments!

The year 2012 is such a time.

We live during an abortion epidemic in the USA that has snuffed
out the lives of 55 million children since 1974

150

and continues even now to kill more than 3000 children every
day – a total greater than the number who died
in the terrorist attack on 9/11.

We live at a time when the leader of Iran (the country where
Esther once lived) has vowed to wipe Israel off the map
and is hurrying to produce nuclear weapons to do just that.

We live at a time when half of all our nation's children are being
born out of wedlock,
when many are saying marriage is obsolete,
and when polls record a majority of people now favor
gay marriage.

Like it or not, we live 'at such a time as this'!

Maybe it is such a time in your personal life.
Some of you face a crisis on a smaller scale, but one that is
personally frightening to you.

You find drug paraphernalia in your teen's dresser drawer.

A friend cries out to you for help, and you fear he may be
suicidal.

You stumble upon some terrible secret at the place where you
work,
like the man who worked for the Parking Violations Bureau in
New York City who discovered a bribery ring that included his
boss, among others.

Behind many of life's critical moments is the menace of some sin
that started SMALL but has begun to grow, and now threatens to
sweep away a whole family
a whole business
a whole congregation.

The Book of Esther is about such a moment.

It also shows us that at such moments,
  God often raises up A KEY PERSON who sees the danger looming
  and is in a position to do something to stop it.

  "It is YOU!" said Mordecai to Esther.
    "You are the queen. You alone are in a position to intercede
    with the king."

  **Who knows whether YOU have come to the kingdom for such a
  time as this?**

Of course, you say, he would point to ESTHER. She was a LEADER.
  And those of us who are LEADERS in our circles must sit up and take
  notice...
            teachers and principals,
          work supervisors, athletic coaches,
        pastors of local congregations.

    We trust such leaders to spot troubles and face them.
      Penn State football Coach Joe Paterno was fired
      because he did not act decisively against an assistant coach
      who molested children.

Leaders are to play a key role. Yes.

But so must others!   Maybe that key person is YOU!

  You say you are a relatively unimportant person?
    Ah, maybe God has put you where you are
    FOR SUCH A TIME AS THIS!

  In an army the sentry on patrol is not as powerful as the GENERAL,
    yet the fate of the general and the whole army may rest on the
    sentry's vigilance.

152

God has made each of us a SENTRY guarding some small part of His world.

You may be the first to see some sin, some danger erupt – and the only one in a position to help.

Remember the story of the Dutch boy
who spied a hole in the dike near his town?
He knew there was no time to ride into town and warn everyone – and he saw no one else around to help.

So he himself knelt down, plugged the hole with his fingers, and waited for help!

Has God put you where you are FOR SUCH A TIME AS THIS?

It may be your task
to plug the hole caused by an ugly rumor, or
to speak out against some dishonest practice at work.

Esther was that key person.
The danger to her people was obvious.
The need to do something was critical.

Should she go in – unbidden – to see the king?
If she did, she would have to take a frightful risk.

For if he did not extend his scepter to her, she would die,
and it had been a month (a month!) since he had sent for her.

Maybe he was angry with her. If so, she'd be a fool to go in.

To accept the responsibility to be God's representative at a crucial moment
may bring us face to face with danger, as it did for Esther.

Have you heard the story of Karen Silkwood,

a worker at a plant that manufactured nuclear fuel rods?

She saw dishonest practices at the factory that would
endanger the public.

But should she risk her own personal safety
to become a whistle blower?
She plunged ahead.
Gathered evidence.
Set out in her car to see a reporter.

But her life ended in a mysterious car crash
and the evidence she had painstakingly gathered
was never found.

Such dangers make us hesitant,
prompt us to wait for a clear sign from God that says, "GO!"

I will do this IF I AM ABSOLUTELY SURE.
If I can say, "I heard a voice! Saw a vision!"

That brings us to a striking element in this story.
There is no mention of God,
not one occurrence of His name,
in the entire book!

Scholars have debated why this is so.
Is the writer of this book portraying life as it often feels to us?
For there are times, aren't there, when God is SILENT, His will
HIDDEN.

There is no Voice that speaks to Esther,
no dream, no heavenly vision.
Only Uncle Mordecai warning,
If you keep silence at such a time as this,
deliverance will arise for the Jews from another quarter,
but you...will perish.

154

"No, Esther," says Mordecai. "God is not absent.
He is waiting on you in this crucial hour. You are to be his hands,
his voice!"

Esther trusts his words.
She orders a three-day fast.
Her way of acknowledging that GOD must direct her.

"God may be hidden from my sight," she seems to say,
"yet I now place myself in His hands and endeavor to obey Him."

If I perish, I perish!

On the third day,
the heavy, ivory-paneled door to the king's chamber swings open,
and Esther enters trembling to see the king.

It is a heart-stopping moment...
a moment in which Esther reminds me of Someone Else
who took His life in His hands to save His people.

Esther finds a striking parallel in JESUS CHRIST.
He too came on the scene at a crucial moment the Bible calls
the fulness of time.

His people were facing death.
He too found the finger pointed squarely at Him:
You! You are my beloved Son.

He too faced a fearful decision that summoned Him to forfeit
His life.

And from Him, likewise, God's face was hidden.
There was no encouraging voice on that Good Friday.
No vision. No angels came to the cross.
Why have you forsaken me? He cried,
but got no answer.

But see what followed for both of them!

Esther found the mercy of the King, who extended his scepter to her.
There came rescue for her people.

Jesus found the mercy of His Father, the great King, who on the third day reached out His hand and raised His Son from death.
And there came rescue for all of us!

And what about you and me in such a time and such a place as this?
Has our courage failed? Our commitment wavered?
Have we kept silence and done nothing...when all depended on us?

Don't be afraid.
Jesus came to forgive the failures and open new doors.

Don't be afraid.
For you and I are not alone.
Our Lord goes ahead of us at just such times as May 13, 2012.

As God directs us, let us rouse ourselves and take a stand.
Let us take our cue from Esther, who placed herself in the hands of God.

Let us pray what we sang together a few minutes ago...
God of grace and God of glory
On your people pour your power
Grant us wisdom, grant us courage
For the facing of this hour,
for the facing of this hour!

KING OF THE HILL
Psalm 2

_____

Picture this.
>It's Sunday morning at a Midwestern church.
>The worship service has ended and the adults stand talking
>>at the church door.

>Meanwhile, out back, a group of boys is playing.

There among the trees behind the church sits a gigantic boulder
nearly six feet high.
>One boy has climbed atop it, and stands there defiant,
>while two or three others are scrambling up to push him off.

Their game is called 'King of the Hill,' and I remember it well,
>for I was one of the boys playing out there on that rock.

For us it was a GAME.

>But for many people, KING OF THE HILL is a way of life!

For them, life is a contest of wills,
>a strenuous climb to the top of one's class
>or to first place in league standings.

It's a race to the top of the corporate ladder to be NUMBER ONE --
>even if it means pushing others aside
>and trampling on them to get there!

This morning, I invite you to stop a moment, look around, and think...
>Where am I on life's HILL?
>>At the bottom?
>>>On top?
>>>>Scrambling up the side?

WHO is to be 'King of the Hill'?

The Psalm for today invites such reflection, for it speaks of a HILL, and of a KING on that hill.
> It even lets us eavesdrop on the restless, angry whisperings of some who would like to bump him off.

> Just listen.
> **READ PSALM 2**

Though written 3000 years ago,
> this Psalm captures a mood increasingly prevalent in the USA -
> a restless, rebellious mood that says, in a hundred different ways,
> **LET US BURST THEIR BONDS...CAST THEIR CORDS FROM US!**

In other words,
> "I'm gonna bust loose! No one's gonna stop me!"

So says the teenager who's tired of his parents and their rules,
> who'd like to leave home and go roam, have his own money and be his own boss.

> Billy Joel sang it this way:
> > *I don't care what you say any more ...this is MY LIFE.*
> > *Go ahead with your own life – LEAVE ME ALONE!*

LET US BURST THEIR BONDS...

So says the middle-aged man or woman
> who's had it up to here with responsibilities,
> who's tired of the 'bonds and cords'
> > of marriage and parenting
> > and punching in at work day after day...

> It happens in the corporate world and in churches too.
> > Years ago a Lutheran pastor quit his position, and ran away with the church organist and quite a lot of the church's money.

158

LET US CAST THEIR CORDS FROM US!

There's a rebellious spirit in our land,
aimed not merely at mom and dad, not merely at social tradition,
   but at GOD HIMSELF!
      It is His cords that people would like to cut...

Take time to read, and to listen.
   You will hear voices railing against the church,
      and against RELIGION ITSELF.

   In some places, the frontal assault on God and the church is brazen,
      even breath-taking.

   Think of the efforts underway to remove even the most general
   references to religious faith from the public square,
      and to muzzle Christians
      who want to pray or witness to people around them.

There's more.

   During its 1993 march on Washington, the homosexual community
   made seven demands,
      one of which was the stifling of any negative teaching or
      preaching on the issue by pastors.

   In a speech to the National Newspaper Association in Atlanta,
      media mogul Ted Turner declared the Ten Commandments
      'obsolete,' and then went further.

      Declaring himself the 'News King,' he proposed ten
      commandments of his own to replace the old ones.

   Ted Turner thinks he is the new Moses! The KING OF THE HILL!

He isn't alone.
   To an increasing number of people,

religion means RESTRAINT
It means cords and shackles, hysteria, homophobia,
medieval narrow-mindedness, and old-fashioned stupidity.

So they work to silence GOD whenever they hear His voice.

In this grown-up version of King of the Hill
they'd bump God off and sit on top themselves.

Let me ask you a very PERSONAL QUESTION.
Have YOU joined that rebellion?

Don't answer that too quickly.

The greatest threat to the Christian faith in this country
is NOT that God's name might be removed from public places,
nor that prayer be removed from public schools,
but that God and His Word would be ignored and denied
in our CHURCHES,
and in the HOMES and the HEARTS of people
who claim to be Christians.

Ours is a quiet, passive sort of rebellion...

"Of course I still have my faith," the rebel says.
But he has stopped going to church because it interferes with his
chosen lifestyle, his hobbies, and his pursuit of money.

"I still believe," she insists,
but she has not read her Bible in years, and her prayers are little
more than perfunctory pauses before meals.

"I still go to church," says another of these quiet rebels,
but he has long ago stopped obeying what the Bible says
because it is inconvenient, or costly, or humiliating.

"If I don't do as I please," she thinks,

"I'll miss my chance at happiness"

"If I give that much," he calculates,
    "I'll wind up with nothing."

"If I love my enemies," they reason,
    "they will walk all over me – they'll wind up on top."

That, indeed, is what this Psalm asks us to consider:
    WHO IS TO BE KING OF THE HILL IN MY LIFE?

And it brings answer.

    There is room for only one at the top of that hill and the spot is
    occupied!

JESUS is the KING ON THAT HILL.

    He has been personally installed there by God.
    I HAVE SET MY KING ON ZION, MY HOLY HILL God says.

Jesus was anointed KING at the Jordan River,
    not with olive oil, like that poured on Queen Elizabeth's head by the
    Archbishop of Canterbury,
        but with the Holy Spirit, as God the Father spoke the
        words of this very Psalm for all to hear:

        YOU ARE MY BELOVED SON!

He was enthroned 'on a hill far away' where stood an old rugged
cross.
    Pontius Pilate announced it on a placard above his head –
        JESUS OF NAZARETH, KING OF THE JEWS

And it was on a HILL where that same Jesus, now risen from the dead,
    met with his dumbfounded disciples and gave them and us the
    marching orders we still follow:

Make disciples of all nations!

For KING He was.
   And KING He still is NOW.
      And KING He shall be evermore, by God's unchanging decree.

   I believe it. Do you?
   Do our lives reflect it?

Centuries turn. Empires come and go.
   The Berlin Wall crumbles. Saddam's statue tumbles.
      The nations rage. People shake their fists...
      AND HE IS STILL KING!

In the 3rd century AD, the Roman Emperor Diocletian
   unleashed the longest and most terrifying persecution against
   the Christian Church ever witnessed in history

   "The name of Jesus is being extinguished," he boasted.
      He had coins minted that bore the inscription:
         "The Christian religion is destroyed!"

But that persecution only spread the church.
   In the end it was Diocletian's empire that crumbled,
   and Jesus who remained KING OF THE HILL.

What MADNESS to rebel against God!

Why do the nations rage? asks the psalm.
   He who dwells in heaven will laugh them to scorn!

Ringing down through history is the laughter of God at the foolish
attempts of men
   to bump Him off the throne...

   The printing press from which Voltaire's infidel works were
   published to attack the church

162

was later used to print Bibles.

GOD LAUGHED!

A prominent British philosopher predicted the death of Christianity
within 20 years,
    but the first meeting of the Bible Society of Edinburgh
    was held in the very room where the philosopher died!

GOD LAUGHED!

One day God will stop the laughing and begin the JUDGMENT
    of all those who have rebelled against Him.

Therefore, you kings, be wise! the Psalm counsels…

But when Jesus came into the world,
    He did not come to laugh at us, nor to condemn us.

No, rather his first purpose was to love us,
even in the midst of our rebellion.
    He came down behind enemy lines, and gave his life in payment
    for our sins and follies.

Alongside the tough words or warning in this Psalm,
    there are also tender words of invitation.
        Lay down your arms!   Cease your rebellion.
        Serve the Lord…kiss his feet…take refuge in him!

TAKE REFUGE, my friend.

When life turns vicious,
    when your hill-climbing is interrupted by an avalanche of troubles,
    put your trust in Him.

A few years back there was a movie about a small boy
    who was continually harassed at school by bigger boys.

At last, in desperation, he found one great big boy and offered to
 pay him to be his personal bodyguard.
 The bigger boy agreed, and the little fellow was safe at last!

TAKE REFUGE IN JESUS, for he came not to bully you but to save you.
 You need not pay him. He did it freely.

TAKE REFUGE IN HIM!
 That means stop climbing, and start kneeling.
 When you do, you will find
 a joy and satisfaction those desperate climbers never discover.

 In Acts 4 we read that when the early Christians were faced
 with threats by King Herod,
 they remembered the words of this Psalm, knelt
 down, and took refuge in their King, Jesus, asking his help.

 The Bible tells us that the building was shaken,
 as God laughed for joy and strengthened those believers.

Jesus still reigns!

 Not too many years ago, in the city of Moscow,
 a Communist party education minister named Lunatcharsky was
 delivering a stinging attack on God and faith to a large, silent
 audience.
 The Christian religion, he asserted, had been overthrown, the
 Bible disproved.
 He challenged anyone in the audience
 to disagree with what he said.

 A single figure rose and came forward.
 It was a young Russian Orthodox priest.
 He stopped, turned to the audience,
 and shouted the Easter greeting, "CHRIST IS RISEN!"

 With one accord, the vast audience roared,

"HE IS RISEN INDEED!"

The priest turned to Lunatcharsky and said in a quiet voice, "I have nothing more to say."

What more needs to be said?

JESUS IS THE KING OF THE HILL!
   Take refuge in him.
   Then, whatever comes, you may laugh and sing for joy.

IT KEEPS ON TICKING
Psalm 136

(The congregation has earlier recited the psalm antiphonally)

Do you remember John Cameron Swayzee?

He's the fellow who, a generation ago, did TIMEX watch
commercials on TV.

I remember one of them vividly.
He fastened a watch to the propeller of an outboard motor.
He lowered it into a clear glass tank of water and started the
motor.
The propeller churned the water into a froth of bubbles.
The motor was stopped and the watch retrieved.
The camera zoomed in to show that the watch was still running.

Then came Swayzee's memorable punch line:
"IT TAKES A LICKING AND KEEPS ON TICKING!"

This morning I want to show you something else that does the same
thing.
Something that, like a good old TIMEX watch, keeps ticking
faithfully as the centuries pass,
something strong and reliable, and infinitely more valuable than
a Timex watch.

I proclaim to you the great gift of God that is the center and subject of
Psalm 136:
Give thanks to the Lord, for He is good,
for His steadfast love endures forever!

Earlier this morning, as we recited this Psalm, you proclaimed it to
each other:
His steadfast love endures forever.

167

26 times, in fact, you repeated it:
His steadfast love endures forever.

Why so much repetition?

The Psalmist wants to drive home a lesson.
He says there's a GIFT God gave you.
Do you realize IT?

Let me illustrate.
Imagine that a wealthy man gave his daughter a valuable cup and saucer made of the finest china,
but found, weeks later, that she was using the cup
as an ashtray and the saucer as the cat's dish!

That man would sit his daughter down and explain to her
the VALUE of that cup and saucer - and their proper use!

In the same way, by means of this psalm,
God takes us by the hand, sits us down, and says:
TAKE A CLOSER LOOK.
APPRECIATE WHAT YOU HAVE.
LEARN TO USE IT ARIGHT!

Very well, then. Let's look more closely at this gift from God.

STEADFAST LOVE.

The Hebrew word is *chesed.*
Translators can't agree on how to translate that word.

The ESV in our hymnals calls it 'steadfast love.'
The NIV renders it as 'love.'
Some other Bibles lengthen that to 'loving-kindness'
to show that it's not merely a feeling,
but something enacted.

The King James used a word many of us grew up with –
'mercy.'
'Mercy' means releasing sinners from a punishment
they richly deserved:
His mercy endureth forever.

If you really wanted to capture this word, it might take a long
phrase, something like
"GOD'S STEADFAST,
UNDESERVED
COVENANT LOVE IN ACTION"!

But even the best definition isn't enough,
so the Psalmist takes us back to the beginning, to give us a slide
show of action pictures
that will portray what this STEADFAST LOVE is all about...

First, it was a CREATING love.
Give thanks to him, the Psalmist bids us,
WHO ALONE DOES GREAT WONDERS
WHO BY HIS UNDERSTANDING MADE THE HEAVENS
WHO SPREAD OUT THE EARTH UPON THE GREAT WATERS
WHO MADE THE GREAT LIGHTS –
THE SUN TO GOVERN THE DAY,
THE MOON AND STARS TO GOVERN THE NIGHT

In a few swift strokes, we see how that steadfast love set the
universe ticking.

Back in 1859 someone published a tract that marveled at the solar
system this way:
There are no iron belts or bars to hold the planets in their
courses. Freely in space they move, poised, balancing, ever in
motion, fulfilling with unerring dignity their mighty cycles, one
grand piece of celestial machinery.

But God is more than a Watchmaker!

He is a loving Father who made, not merely stars or planets,
but PEOPLE too!

Rivaling the mystery of the worlds 'out there'
is the world 'in here' within the heart and mind
of a human being.

We are, says another Psalm, **fearfully and wonderfully made**.

And God, who is more than a Watchmaker, did more than set it all
ticking.
Day after day He sustains us.
Year after year, century after century,
He feeds and renews His whole Creation.

How does one USE such a message?

Shouldn't it provoke us to a daily TRUST in His care?

Edward Taylor, the famed sailor preacher of Boston, was about
to embark on a long ocean voyage to Europe.
He admitted he was worried about
how his congregation would fare in his absence.

But one Sunday morning, as he stood at the altar praying,
he suddenly interrupted his prayer and exclaimed to his people,
What am I saying?
Do I distrust the providence of heaven?
A God who gives a whale a ton of herring for a breakfast, will
He not care for my children here?

Yes, He will! For **His steadfast love endures forever**.
You and I may claim that promise too.

Isn't that why, in years past, many parents taught their children
to pray these psalm words after every meal?

O give thanks unto the Lord, for He is good, for His mercy endureth forever.

Every meal, after all, is a reminder that
    HIS LOVE KEEPS ON TICKING.

But there's much more to this story.
    History records that, like the TIMEX watch on that propeller,
        the divine love that keeps on ticking
        has taken a mighty LICKING at the hands of sinful people.

Who can forget the Bible stories we learned already as children –
    the jealousy and murder of Cain?
        the complaining of the Israelites in the wilderness?
        the adultery of David?
          the night when Peter denied His Lord?

God's LOVE takes a LICKING from every one of us!
    How many lies have we told?
      How many angry words have we blurted out?
      How persistently we've bowed to the Almighty Dollar,
        misused sex, gotten drunk,
        and worried ourselves toward an early grave?

Or would you say otherwise?

A pastor was visiting a man who objected that he was not, after all,
a very great sinner.
    "Do you sin at all?" the pastor asked him.

"Oh, a little, I guess," the man admitted,
    "maybe 2-3 times a day."

"Only 3 sins a day?" the pastor mused. "But in a year that makes
    a thousand. And in a lifetime, 70,000!"

70,000?!

Even from the best of us, God's steadfast love takes a licking!
But look, says the Psalmist: "It keeps right on TICKING!"

The next set of verses chronicle the REDEEMING LOVE of God,
   the story of how God rescued a nation of rebels:

   O give thanks, He bids us, give thanks to Him who
      STRUCK DOWN THE FIRSTBORN OF EGYPT
      AND BROUGHT ISRAEL OUT FROM AMONG THEM
         WITH A MIGHTY HAND AND AN OUTSTRETCHED ARM
      WHO DIVIDED THE RED SEA ASUNDER
         AND BROUGHT ISRAEL THROUGH THE MIDST OF IT
      WHO LED HIS PEOPLE THROUGH THE DESERT
      WHO STRUCK DOWN GREAT KINGS –
         SIHON, KING OF THE AMORITES,
         AND OG, KING OF BASHAN

   This Og was no historical footnote, no small potatoes!
      He was, the Bible records, a gigantic man who would dwarf
      Shaquille O'Neal,
         an enormous man who slept on an iron bedstead
         nine feet long!

   But God's rescuing love routed Og as if he were a pygmy
   and delivered Israel.

Do you think your giant enemies will fare any better when God deals
with them –
   those awful addictions,
      those humiliating habits,
         those stubborn sins,
            that dreadful death you face?

For DEAL WITH THEM HE HAS!

   That steadfast love did not stop once Israel was safely settled into
   Canaan.

172

It KEPT ON TICKING down through the centuries.
He sent kings to shepherd those people,
prophets to correct them and give them hope,
and last and best of all HIS SON.

Son of David, have mercy on me!
cried out a blind man to Him,
for that was what he needed, what we all need – that
STEADFAST, UNDESERVED COVENANT LOVE IN ACTION!

And that's what Jesus delivered.
It wasn't easy, for Jesus took a LICKING at our hands.

We called Him names,
tested him with trick questions to catch Him in His words,
picked up stones to throw at Him,
taunted Him, spit on Him, crucified Him.

But look!
He kept on ticking God's mighty heartbeat of love...
Be of good cheer – your sins are forgiven!
Neither do I condemn you!
Truly you will be in paradise with me!

Even nails and spear and the grave itself could not stop that mighty
steadfast love.
It emerged from the tomb on Easter morning,
still beating its rhythm of mercy.

There is not a rich person on earth that could afford to buy
a single moment of God's MERCY.
Yet because of Jesus,
the poorest among us is promised all he needs,
to be received simply by believing it.

When the great Thomas Hooker was dying,
one of his friends said,

"Now you are going to receive the rewards of your long labors."

"No," replied Hooker. "I am going to receive MERCY!"

That's why we've come here, isn't it?
    For <u>we</u> need mercy too!

    Maybe, just maybe, you are tired of ASKING.
    Maybe, you fear, God may get tired of GIVING.

If so, hear these words again: **His STEADFAST LOVE LASTS FOREVER!**

It lasts, like nothing else on earth.

    Every creature has its appointed life span.
        Most insects are here a single summer.
        A beloved pet dog or cat – maybe 15 years.
        People may live 100 years,
            and those giant redwoods and sequoias a thousand or two.

        But all creatures die.

    All our best machines will finally wear out too.
        My auto is chugging toward 100,000 miles, showing its age.
        Energizer batteries and, alas, even Timex watches finally quit!

But there IS one thing...one thing alone in all the world...that
    takes a licking and keeps on ticking to all eternity:

    THAT STEADFAST LOVE OF GOD IN JESUS CHRIST!

Aren't you glad?!

    Don't be discouraged by your sins, no matter how stubborn.
        WHY? (Say it with me)
            HIS STEADFAST LOVE LASTS FOREVER!

174

Don't be disheartened by a wicked world and a faltering church.
WHY? (Say it again)
HIS STEADFAST LOVE LASTS FOREVER!

That love is at work in you, people!
And in all who know Jesus by faith.

Take a good look at what God has given you. (Once more)
HIS STEADFAST LOVE LASTS FOREVER!

Appreciate it.
Give thanks for it.
And above all, use it!

You can't wear it out.

Not ever.

It keeps on ticking.

APPLES OF GOLD
Proverbs 25:11-15

(delivered on Sunday School Rally Day)

Read the TEXT

I like the word APPLE. A simple, wholesome word.

It transports me to my back yard, where I can stand beneath my own
    beautiful trees – a Gravenstein and a Fuji.

It takes me back in time to my boyhood in Indiana,
    when I worked on Saturdays at the Adrian Orchards, pumping cider
    and selling apples by the bag and the half-bushel – apples with
    crisp, cheerful names like
        Jonathan, MacIntosh, Winesap, and Rome Beauty.

But the apple the Bible holds up before us this morning
    is not the fruit of a tree. It is the fruit of the MOUTH:
    A word fitly spoken is like apples of gold in a setting of silver.

Let's consider this picture together, for all of us use words every day.
    Here God will teach us how the words we speak may be 'fitting'
    words – simple, wholesome words –
        APPLES OF GOLD.

Start with that word GOLD.

Golden things are rare, and very precious.
    But most words are neither!

    Rare? We are deluged, overwhelmed
        with an avalanche of words day after day.

    If I can believe what I read, the average person speaks between

10,000 and 25,000 words a day – enough to fill a small booklet!

What's more, the average person is exposed to about 1500
commercial messages (ads) every day –
    on billboards, in newspapers, on TV, radio, and the internet.

Precious?
In an essay, a high school boy named Tom complained:

> *Words are everywhere.*
> *People spit them out all the time,*
> *and most of the time, they are wasted.*
> *There are millions of words spinning through the air,*
> *crashing against each other, and saying nothing!*

Because of this daily verbal barrage, many of us have come to think
that what would be really golden is SILENCE!

It takes a fine command of language to say nothing --
    to learn to keep our mouths shut when we would rather
    prattle on and on!

What if words were RATIONED?

Can you imagine what it would be like if each person were allowed
    to speak, say, just 100 words a day?
        WE MIGHT BE MORE CAREFUL!

We would weigh our words, consider carefully WHAT to say...
    and WHEN... and to WHOM!

Words would suddenly become more precious,
    and perhaps more GOLDEN.

But even then, we would finally have to ask, "What shall we say?"
    When we speak, what words would God have us use?

Here in Proverbs 25, there are three different kinds of 'apple words' held before us.

The first is in verse 12:

**Like a gold ring or an ornament of gold is
a wise reprover to a listening ear.**

The first golden apple is the word of REPROOF or REBUKE.

God holds it before us because this word is one we normally shrink from speaking.
Correcting someone's behavior is painful,
and most of us do not willingly say such things to each other.

Newly-married couples, still immersed in their dream world, want to be very careful.

Friends, family members, and fellow church-goers usually choose to store up angry feelings instead of speaking an open rebuke.

Alas, when we do finally rebuke someone, it may be because we have lost our patience... can't hold it in any longer!
So the word is spoken, but not very 'fitly.'

It will be delivered with a smug superiority that belittles another,
or with an angry sharpness that stabs someone like a knife.

HAVE YOU WITNESSED SUCH VERBAL EXPLOSIONS?
DELIVERED ONE YOURSELF?

What makes the apple of reproof a golden apple, says Proverbs, is if it is 'wise.'
The wise will pray first, asking God for the right words,
and for the right time when such words can be
rightly heard and pondered.

The wise person is not satisfied to say, "Well, at least it's the truth," but will ask further,

"How may I speak this truth IN LOVE?"

Those who receive such a golden apple of reproof
  may be helped toward repentance
  and real CHANGE in their lives.

   During the fourth year of our marriage, after Sue and I had been
   through our worst fight,
      she delivered to me a GOLDEN APPLE – a word fitly spoken at a
      time I most needed it –
         a word that rebuked my selfishness
         and pleaded for me to treat her as a wife and not
            as a maid to do my chores.

   WISE, LOVING REPROOF IS A GOLDEN APPLE.

The second is the word of PERSUASION.

   It is described in verse 15:
      **With patience a ruler may be persuaded, and a soft tongue
      will break a bone.**

Here God urges us to be responsible citizens,
   speaking words to shape policies and influence choices, especially
   as we address our leaders,
      the people who have power to make such decisions.

   This Golden Apple may be spoken at an open hearing
      where a community considers a highway bypass
      or at a school board meeting where there is discussion of a new
         sex education curriculum

   Here God is also urging us to be responsible CHURCH MEMBERS
      who aren't afraid to voice needs and feelings
      as the congregation charts its course.

   This Golden Apple may be delivered to a pastor in his study,

or at a gathering of the voters,
      as the congregation discusses a facility expansion
      or the use of a new hymnal.

We need this word from God about the Golden Apple of persuasion
      because too many of us opt out and let 'somebody else' do it
      both in the public arena and in the church.

      Those who DO speak often do more to damage things than to help,
      for they grow impatient for change they think comes too slowly.

      Meetings and conversations turn into verbal fistfights
            as we try to pummel opponents into submission
            and make them say,
                  "I give up….you're right!"

Does it work that way?
      Don't we find just the opposite – that an angry opponent
      will make us stiffen our resistance?

            How many parents who truly want the best for their children
            have tried to force their obedience with harsh words and stiff
            consequences,
                  only to have them resist and rebel?

            Some of the most stubborn, angry teens come out of homes
            where the parents chose to be enforcers rather than
            persuaders.

If we are to persuade, this 'apple' will be golden only if it is PATIENT
and GENTLE.

      Patient.
            William Wilberforce, the man who almost single-handedly
            brought an end to the British slave trade, did it with patience.
                  It took twenty years of speech-making to Parliament
                  before he saw any results!

Gentle.
   During the Reformation, Martin Luther came to realize
   that he was too crude and forceful in his language,
      so he urged his co-worker, Philip Melanchthon, to
      do some of the writing for him.

   Of Melanchthon, he said,
      I cannot tread so gently as Master Philip.

Gentle, patient persuasion is a golden apple.

Now for the third and final one. It appears in verse 13:
   **Like the cold of snow in the time of harvest is a faithful messenger
   to those who sent him.   He refreshes the spirit of his masters.**

The third GOLDEN APPLE is the word that brings
an important MESSAGE.

   God would have us be MESSENGERS,
      deliverers of important NEWS
      that will make both the sender and the receiver glad.

Most news doesn't!
   Famine in Africa and Asia because of soaring food prices.
      Growing warfare in Afghanistan as Iraq winds down.
         Another evacuation mess for Gulf Coast residents.
         Political mud-slinging in this election year.

   What we hear on the evening news and read in the papers day by
   day is often more rotten than refreshing.
      Hatred! Greed! Vulgarity!

In the middle of it all, God holds before us the last and best of His
Golden Apples,
   Good News straight from Heaven, a special message for an unhappy
   world –

Unto you is born this day in the city of David... a SAVIOR!

'Change you can believe in' was not minted on the presidential trail in 2008.

> It was invented by God and sent to earth
> in the person of Jesus Christ,
>> who is able to deliver changed hearts to those who trust Him
>> and who, at the last day,
>>> will change our lowly bodies to be like His.

Surely this is the sweetest thing one human being can tell another.
> I have seen it move grown men and women to tears right before my eyes.

What a word!

But will it be 'fitly spoken' by the messengers - spoken with conviction and joy
> in words that worldly ears can understand?

> Most of all, will it be spoken by messengers
> whose lives do not contradict the message they bring?

> When a pastor is ordained, he is asked,
>> *Will you adorn the doctrine of our Savior with a godly life?*

> There are pastors who don't.
>> A friend of mine lamented that he had a hard time listening to his pastor because whenever the pastor sat with the men of the church, he told one filthy joke after another.
>>> "I expect more from my pastor," he said.

> I pray that, in my own ministry, my sins and weaknesses
> do not tarnish this golden apple for you.

How about you?

Does the way you live
    drown out the word you want to speak about Jesus?

Would you say that the fruits that issue from your mouth
    are the golden apples God summons you to speak?

If not, stop to consider that
    what COMES OUT of our mouths closely resembles
    what GOES IN to our ears.

The word we speak is fertilized by the WORD WE HEAR.

    The first-grader spouting profanity has been hearing it somewhere.
    So has the tiny tot who sings songs of praise.

That's why, on this Rally Sunday, we focus so heavily on our Sunday
School and our day school
    as places where children may hear the Good News of Jesus,
    so that they will be equipped to speak that Good News too.

    Some years ago in Sequim, Washington, where we used to live,
        a teenaged girl won an award called the Golden Apple Award.

    It is presented to anyone who commits to memory the entire
    Book of Proverbs.

    She had done that! An amazing accomplishment.

    I knew that young lady, and I can tell you truly
        that the Word she read and memorized was reflected in the
        words she spoke every day – gracious godly words!

We teach the Word written in the Bible,
    for within those words is the one great Word – Him whose name is
    'The Word.'
    Jesus, the Word made flesh who
        dwelt among us, full of grace and truth.

184

When He came, God held out the Golden Apple to us –
   to taste and eat and digest.

   This is not the FORBIDDEN FRUIT that brought Adam and Eve
   misery.

   This is the PERMITTED FRUIT from God's own Tree of Life.

I hold it out to you this morning.

I speak to you, as fitly as I know how, this Golden Apple
   that is the News of Jesus your Savior and Lord.

   I proclaim to you this message that God loved you in the midst of
   your sins,
      and sent His Son to bear them all and free you.

The most Golden of Apples!

   Hear it well.
   Taste it again...and again!

      Then, increasingly, you will speak it.

WHISTLING WHILE YOU WORK
Ecclesiastes 2:24

(A message preached on Labor Day)

The Seven Little Men got ready for work, as they did every day.
They put on their pants, shirts, and hoods.
They tightened their belts.
Each took his pick-axe and swung it to his shoulder.

Off to the mine they marched in a line, singing as they went,
Hi Ho, Hi Ho, it's off to work we go...

At the window, watching them go, was Snow White.
As the dwarfs disappeared down the road, she went to her own
tasks with a song to her animal helpers:
Just whistle while you work...
And cheerfully together we can tidy up the place.
So hum a merry tune ...
It won't take long when there's a song to help you set the pace!

I hold that picture before you today
not as a bit of escapist entertainment, but as a serious example to
imitate, for the Bible urges us to do that very thing,
to enjoy our toil,
to whistle while we work!

That's a message woven through the Book of Ecclesiastes.

Listen to what wise Solomon tells us in chapter 2, verse 24 (and
repeats in three other places):
**There is nothing better for a man that that he should eat and
drink and find enjoyment in his toil.**

Enjoy your toil! Whistle while you work!

A fitting piece of advice for a Labor Day weekend, don't you think?

I looked up Labor Day in Wikipedia and learned that
   Labor Day was begun in New York City,
   and later made a federal holiday in 1884.

   It celebrates the American worker...that's us!

Even though it isn't a churchly festival,
   it's a good time for us as the people of God to pause
   before diving in...
      to think about our work and our attitude toward it.

Here's where I'd like you to help me with today's sermon.

In the bulletin, there's a space provided underneath the sermon title.

   Would you take a pencil or pen and write in what <u>your</u> job is?
      Kids, if you are in school, your job is 'being a student.'
      Stay-at-home parents, your very important work is 'Parenting.'
      Retirees, even if you're retired, you likely have some kind of
         work that occupies your time. List it there.

   Now, the key issue. How do you feel about your work?
         LOVE IT?   TOLERATE IT?   CAN'T STAND IT?

   Be truthful about that, and try to supply the reason after the word
   'because'...

The topic of WORK is a big one in the Bible.

God cares not only about your Sabbath day activities,
   but about what you do the other six days of the week!

   Why? Because He made us in His image.
      What He does, we are to do.
      God WORKED six days, then he RESTED.

188

We work all week, then <u>we</u> rest.

And what is that appointed work?
    In Genesis 2, Adam is put in charge of Eden, to **till it and keep it.**
    He was, and we still are, STEWARDS of the earth.

    We are charged with the daily task of caring for the world
    and each other,
        as managers for God.

    Let's take stock of what we do... (hands, please)
        How many are STUDENTS?   TEACHERS?

        Anyone here this morning work in the Health Care industry?
            Law enforcement?   Manufacturing?   Real Estate?
            Computer-related?

        How about others? (tell me...)

Whatever our job, God's intent is that we ENJOY IT.

But there's a problem. Many of us don't.
    Someone has put poisoned apples in our lunch pails!

I'm guessing that for at least some of us, the work day does NOT begin
    with us leaping from bed with a shout of delight
    and whistling as we head out the driveway.

A more frequent scenario might be
that the alarm clock rings, and we groan.
    There comes a hurried breakfast.
        A quick review of the day's lengthy 'to-do list.'
            A commute through snarled traffic,
                and a snide comment from a co-worker
                as we arrive a little later than planned.

Why do we work? Well, because there are bills to pay!

The marching song of the dwarfs has been replaced
with what I saw recently on a bumper sticker:
   I owe, I owe, so off to work I go!

Snow White's whistling is replaced by Tennessee Ernie Ford's
work-day dirge:
   Sixteen tons, and whaddya get?
   Another day older and deeper in debt
   St. Peter, don't you call me 'cause I can't go
   I owe my soul to the company store!

Forget the song. We can say it in plain English.
   Many people don't like their work.
      Or their co-workers.
         Or their bosses.
            Or all of the above.

There's white-collar crime. Drinking on the job. Boredom.
And just plain laziness.

After my HS graduation, I went to work at a warehouse for a summer.
   There I got a quick education about the state of the workplace.

As I pushed my floor-cleaning machine past the railroad dock,
   I found my fellow workers sitting
   in a yet-to-be-unloaded boxcar...
      drinking beers...
   and with them, the unit supervisor, also drinking.

      I looked, dumbfounded.
      They laughed at me, and went on drinking.

Even if we embrace our work and do our best, we face unpleasant
challenges.
   It's hard to fight the traffic.
      Hard to get ahead of the bills.
         Hard to see a noble purpose in what we do day after day.

The Greeks had a story about a fellow named Sisyphus,
who was condemned by the gods to roll a boulder up a hill.

But before he could get it to the top, it would roll back down,
and he had to do it over again...
    and again and again...
    forever.

It feels like that to a lot of people. Maybe to you.

What has gone wrong with work?

The Bible says it happened early on.
    Adam and Eve transgressed the Maker's rules.
    Decided to do it their way, not His.

Just one chapter after Adam is assigned as Eden's care-taker,
he is hauled in before the Boss, who tells his rebellious worker:
    Cursed is the ground because of you!
    In toil shall you eat of it all the days of your life.
    Thorns and thistles it shall bring forth to you...
    In the sweat of your face you shall eat bread
        till you return to the ground.

That's the way it's been ever since.

The problem with our work is the problem that hangs over all our
human endeavors.
    The problem of SIN – our rebellion against the Master
                and our competition with our co-workers.

In Ecclesiastes, Solomon's urging to enjoy our work
is written with resignation,
    for he knows that down here 'under the sun'
    there's much that's out of sync in our daily life and work.

Here are two of the problems, he says.

First, many workers are driven by envy rather than love,
to have more than others rather than to serve them.
Vanity, he says.

Second, there is the uncertainty of the future.
When a man dies, he asks sadly,
who knows whether he will leave all that he has earned
to a wise man or a fool?
Vanity! All is vanity!

Solomon's conclusion? Might as well try and enjoy yourself now,
since there is not much else to look forward to under the sun!

Is there any hopeful word for workers on this Labor Day weekend?

Let's look back at those dwarves for a moment.

There was a reason they went so happily to their work, wasn't there?
She was standing at the door to send them off
and welcome them back.
She worked with a song, and her joy was infectious.

God designed it to be that way for us.
Instead of leaving us alone with our toil and our trouble,
He sent someone to come and live among us –
someone whose presence would put a song in our hearts
no matter what the day might hold.

Jesus came to His holy work alongside us.

Even as a child he had a strong sense of vocation:
Don't you know, He asked his mother,
that I must be about my Father's business?

No, not the carpentry business of his earthly father, Joseph,
though doubtless He did that work cheerfully and well.

192

I mean the business of His heavenly Father –
   the great work of seeking and freeing all of us
   who've had our noses to the Devil's grindstone.

Think of all the things He did to accomplish the Father's
assignment! What a job description...
   He was a STUDENT of Scripture at home.
   He became a TEACHER on hillsides, lakes, and synagogues.
   He did the work of a HEALER for countless sick ones
      and the FEEDER of multitudes.
   All the while He daily MENTORED the Twelve.

Gathered with his disciples in the Upper Room on Maundy
Thursday,
   He prayed a prayer of thanks to His Father that He had
   accomplished the work He had been given...

   a work brought to its gracious completion the next day
   as He offered His life to pay the price,
      to set us free from our slavery
      here 'under the sun.'

It is finished! He said.

"And we are free!" we may now say and sing.

A country boy was listening to sermon about Romans 6:23.
   "The wages of sin is death!" the preacher thundered.

The boy turned to his brother and whispered,
   "Well, if the Devil ain't gonna pay no better than that,
   I ain't gonna work for Him n'more!"

No, and we won't either!
   Not for the Devil as Boss any more.
   Not out of envy or competition any more.
   Not for Death as a paycheck any more.

For we have a new Master.
A gracious one who paid the price for our freedom -
>   who forgives the sins of the workplace
>   who sings a song of love and life in our ears.

And we have a larger vision of the work we do.
For it is no longer simply laying carpet, or grading papers,
>   or baking cakes, or delivering mail...

>   now it has become what it was meant to be –
>   serving one another in love,
>   being the very hands of Christ for our neighbors
>   so that in our work
>   they may MEET HIM!

God's promise, you know, is not just about CHURCH WORK,
but about ALL THE WORK WE DO...
>   **in the Lord your LABOR is not in vain!**

There's an old story about a man who watched the construction of a cathedral in France centuries ago.
>   On one section he saw three stonemasons working on a wall.

"What are you doing?" he asked the first.
>   "I am laying stone," was the man's reply.

"What are you doing?" he asked the second.
>   "I am building a wall," the man said.

"What are you doing?" he asked the third.
>   "Ah," smiled the man, "I am helping to build a cathedral where God will come close to us!"

They were all doing the same thing. Yet not the same!
>   For that last man's work had been taken up
>   into the larger vision of life offered by St. Paul:

194

So whether you eat or drink or whatever you do, do all to the glory of God! (1 Corinthians 10:31)

Look once more at what you wrote on your bulletin a few minutes ago.

   See it in a new way, knowing that Jesus has come to give you
   a new Master
      and a new purpose.

Knowing Him, it will be easier to whistle while you work!

DISAPPOINTMENT WITH GOD
Jeremiah 20:7-13

Have you ever been disappointed?

Ah, silly question!
    There isn't a one of us that hasn't been...again and again.

    The fans hoped their team would win. But it LOST!

    The couple tried for years to have a baby.
       But they remain CHILDLESS.

    The young man who started a business
    and poured his heart and soul and lots of money into it.
       But the business FOLDED.

Yes. We all know about disappointment.
So let me ask a deeper question. A harder one.
    HAVE YOU EVER BEEN DISAPPOINTED WITH GOD?

    Perhaps it seems blasphemous to hear your pastor ask
    a question like this.
       For haven't we come to expect something else in church?

    Let us not speak of disappointment here...   NO!

    Let us speak to one another about the victorious Christian life
                          the triumphs of faith
                   the answered prayers!

      We want to hear about MIRACLES
        and dramatic testimonies of CHANGED LIVES.

Disappointment with God?
    A dangerous topic to address in a sermon!

Nevertheless, I will address it.
Because many people – including some of us –
have experienced it.

Disappointment in PRAYER...
Marge, a woman with two children, learned that both had
cystic fibrosis.
Undaunted by the gloomy predictions of doctors,
she set about praying for healing.

But her children, Joe and Peggy, both died in their early twenties.

Disappointment in MINISTRY...
Every year in our church body and others,
we lose scores of pastors and teachers
who once entered their careers with high hopes
and abundant energy,

but wind up quitting their vocations – bruised by conflict
wounded by vicious personal attacks,
disillusioned by the pettiness and partisanship they
often encounter

There are other disappointments too.

Some of you have told me how your heart breaks for a dear child or
grandchild,
whose picture on your wall reminds you of happier times
when they were young and seemed so close to God.

But now they have drifted away from the church - in some
cases, from faith too - and you cry out:

HAS GOD FORGOTTEN THEM?

WERE OUR EFFORTS AND EXAMPLE ALL IN VAIN?

Long ago there lived a man —
  a good man, a believer, a powerful spokesman for God.
  A man who, in the midst of his prophetic ministry,
  grew disappointed, even disillusioned, with God.

  We know about this man, because he left behind
  his personal diary,
    a book filled with grief and pain.

This man was JEREMIAH,
  and his words have something to teach us about our times of
  disappointment with God. Listen to what he writes...
      READ 15:15-18   and   20:7-10

These words teach us that
  DISAPPOINTMENT NEEDS TO BE EXPRESSED.

  Jeremiah does it repeatedly, powerfully... in writing.

  Woven through his book are astonishingly personal, pain-filled
      words:
          My heart is sick inside me
          Lord, you... deceived me, overpowered me!
          Why is my pain unceasing?
          Cursed be the day I was born!

All this won't surprise you
if you read about the things that happened to him.
    How plots were made against his life.
      How the king took Jeremiah's carefully-written letter,
      cut it in pieces, and burned it.
        How he was beaten, and put in stocks, body bent almost
        double.
          How people avoided him and made fun of him, and how for
          23 years his preaching fell on deaf ears.

Jeremiah was DISAPPOINTED WITH GOD...

and not afraid to say so out loud.   Isn't that a lesson to us?

Too often the CHURCH is a gathering place for PRETENDERS –
   a place where we think we have to look good at all costs!
      There is to be no CRYING in here.
     And certainly no ANGER!

  When asked how we feel, we are supposed to say,
    "Oh, FINE! Everything's just FINE!"

  We give lip service to the general truth of SIN.
    But let no one dare to admit a real, shameful,
    disgusting wrong.
      Let's keep all such things hidden from view!

  "Isn't it sad," someone once told me, "that the place where I go
  to be truly myself, with all my hurts and ugliness, is AL-ANON?
    I really need the support of fellow believers,
    but I don't dare say how I feel
    in here!"

Do YOU dare? Do I?

Jeremiah had the courage to express his disappointment.

But there is more in this text...
  That disappointment needs not only to be EXPRESSED.
  IT NEEDS TO BE EXAMINED.

In chapter 15, when Jeremiah complains, he gets an answer from
God:
If you return, I will restore you, and you shall stand before me.
If you utter what is precious, and not what is worthless, you
shall be as my mouth. They shall turn to you, but you shall not
turn to them. And I will make you to this people a fortified
wall of bronze; they will fight against you, but they shall not
prevail over you, for I am with you to deliver you...

God takes Jeremiah's complaint and holds it before him like a mirror.
As if to say,
"Listen to yourself. Why do you say what you do?"

For God had not failed Jeremiah.
It was not He who had made the plots, or burned the letter.
God had not beaten Jeremiah...
PEOPLE had done all those things.

Let me ask you the same thing, friend.
Is it really GOD who has disappointed you? or is it PEOPLE?

As I listen to the laments of people, I hear stories about
the pastor who didn't listen
the child who rebelled
the spouse who broke a vow
the congregation that turned a deaf ear to someone in
trouble.

"But NO!" someone will say. "It was GOD who failed me!
I prayed. I trusted Him. I tried to follow.
He ignored my prayers!"

But even this needs to be examined.
WHAT IS IT THAT YOU EXPECTED FROM GOD THAT HE DIDN'T
GIVE YOU?

In his book *DISAPPOINTMENT WITH GOD*, author Philip Yancey says
there are three basic complaints people make about God:
a) God is HIDDEN – we never see Him
b) God is SILENT – we cannot hear His voice clearly
c) God is UNFAIR – He does not deal with people in a
consistent way

Perhaps you have felt one or all of these!
If so, let me ask you:
If God took care of all these things, would you be a better

person, a consistently faithful follower?

Don't answer that too fast!
    For once upon a time,
    God did all this for the Israelites in the Wilderness.

    VISIBLE? Sure was!
    In that pillar of cloud or fire in the midst of their camp.

    AUDIBLE? You bet!
    He was always speaking with Moses or booming forth
    on Mt. Sinai. No mistaking that powerful voice!

    FAIR? Indeed so!
    Every rebellion was quickly punished,
    every obedience richly rewarded.

Did all of this make the Israelites a model community of believers?
    Ah, you know the answer!

    You know that they grumbled and griped against Him for 40 years.

    How often we have done the same,
    even when things were going well.
        How often we have broken His fatherly heart.
        How often He could have said to us, "Child, I am so disappointed
        in YOU!"

Let us examine our disappointments
    and see whether in our demands, we are letting GOD be GOD,
    or whether we are clamoring to take His place and run things
        ourselves...

    I've had to learn that in my ministry. I have been disappointed by
                    elders who wouldn't help
                confirmation students who wouldn't study
                programs that fizzled

members who drifted, and by
whole congregations that shrank instead of growing.

I confess: I have been disappointed with GOD!
Didn't he hear my prayers
for those students, those elders, those straying members?

Couldn't He orchestrate a little SUCCESS in there?

Or could it be ME who was in the way of it all
with my pride and immaturity?
Could God Himself be at work in such frustrations,
teaching me patience, love, and understanding?

Yes, DISAPPOINTMENT needs to be expressed...
and, yes, it needs to be examined for its real causes.

But we must not miss the last, best lesson from Jeremiah's life:
IN THE END, GOD HEALS THE DISAPPOINTMENTS
OF THOSE WHO TRUST HIM.

Look again. God did not walk out on Jeremiah. Didn't cut him off.

After the rebuke came a word of comfort.
I will restore you, He said. **I am with you to save you.**

And so he was. The plots against Jeremiah failed.
The prophet lived on 20 more years and finished his work
in faith.
His book was preserved, and his words lived on to inspire
Israel...and US.

700 years after Jeremiah came another
who spoke God's great ASSURANCE:
I AM WITH YOU ALWAYS!
His name was JESUS.
He came expressly to help disappointed people:

Surely he has borne our griefs and carried our sorrows!

VISIBLE? Never before had God been SEEN SO CLEARLY –
    Not in a pillar of fire, but in a man with a face, with eyes
    that cried tears of compassion and hands that embraced the
        untouchables.
    If you have seen me, you have seen the father also.

AUDIBLE? Never before had God spoken so clearly
    of His plan and His will toward human beings.
    I have come to seek and to save the lost, He announced.

    And those who heard Him said,
    No man ever spoke as this man spoke!

FAIR? Never before had God been so fair – yes, more than fair!
    Here in Jesus was pardon and grace for people who deserved
    nothing but punishment.
    This man receives sinners and eats with them!

Jesus took our DISAPPOINTMENTS, carried them to His cross,
    and spoke the anguish of our hearts:
        My God, my God, why have you forsaken me?

God's answer to our DISAPPOINTMENTS was delivered
on Easter morning.
    Jesus lives! His rising is the promise that
    HOPE triumphs over death.

    At the end of the great fantasy trilogy *LORD OF THE RINGS*,
        Sam the Hobbit is surprised to awaken from almost certain
        death and find himself in a comfy bed, looking at the face of
            Gandalf, the wizard he thought was dead.
            What's happened to the world? Sam asks.
            Is everything sad going to come untrue?
            Gandalf laughs and says, *A great shadow has departed.*

204

It's TRUE!
What we proclaim is not a fantasy, but the greatest, truest story
ever told.

The great Shadow of Death and Hell was blown away
on Easter morning.

God's Son lives.
In him, all our disappointments will finally melt away.

Take heart, my friend!
Bring your disappointments to God, and He will heal you.

OUR PLANS AND HIS PLANS
Jeremiah 29:11

(Wedding sermon for my daughter and son-in-law)

———————————————

Today, I must confess,
    though I stand here in the pastor's place,
    I am seeing with a father's eyes.

The bridal gown fades and there before me is a little girl
playing with dolls.

Do you remember, Christa, how you and Melanie transformed
    our basement in Akron into 'Dolltown'?

What struck your mother and me as we watched
is that you did more than PLAY.

You PLANNED.

Each doll, of course, received a NAME.
    Martha and Jana,
    and Clara and Detria and Sietta.

But that was only the beginning.

You gave each doll a family history.
    For each one you planned out a whole life,
    complete with baptisms and weddings and babies,
        and, yes, an occasional kidnapping or death,
        for which I could be called on to provide a funeral!

You planned everything for those dolls.

When you grew up, you kept on making plans.

But now, instead of your dolls,
    it was your own life you were planning.

Remember?
    You planned to become a teacher – a teacher of the gifted –
    and have a parallel career as a writer.

Naturally, you planned to marry and have children of your own.

Where would you live?
    You made plans for a large house with secret rooms
    connected by hidden passageways.

Such wonderful, romantic dreams!

Jeff, I didn't get to watch you grow up, but I know you had plans too.
    One of those plans was to become
    a Director of Christian Education in a church.

To realize that plan, you enrolled at Concordia College in Portland.

It was there that your plans and Christa's plans intersected.
    It wasn't long before a NEW PLAN was forming –
    a plan for this wonderful wedding day!

What painstaking detail went into the planning for today:
    the names of the wedding party,
        the engraving of the glasses,
            the food for the reception, the flowers, the photographer...

Ah, and there are still more plans for what will follow:
    your honeymoon trip to Disneyland,
        the move to a rental home on Junior Street in Portland,
        where Christa will finish her education to become a teacher,
            and after that another move to Florida,
            where Jeff will finish his schooling.

So many plans!

But now, for a few minutes, I ask you to lay it all aside.
    Lay aside the PLANNING, and do some LISTENING
    to the Word of God, who says to you in Jeremiah 29:11:
        I know the plans I have for you, says the Lord;
        plans for good and not for evil, to give you a future and a hope.

Hear those words well.

Today God looks down on you two,
    just as you, Christa, once looked down on your Dolltown...

    but with this difference —
        you are not dolls to him, but living people,
        His own dear children!

On this day, you are stopping to stand before Him,
    to listen to His Word
    and to acknowledge that His plans are the ones that matter most.

For you see — and this is the hard word I must speak to you —
    GOD'S plans are not always the same as YOUR plans.

    The Israelites learned that the hard way.

    These words from Jeremiah 29
        were spoken to the people of Israel at the beginning
        of their Exile to Babylon.

    For the Israelites, normal life had been derailed by disaster.
        They had lost a war...and as a result, they lost their HOMES
                                                    their LAND
                                    and their FREEDOM.
        Their temple was burned to ashes.
        Their king led away in chains.

It wasn't at all what they had planned!

Many of them were forced to move away,
  settle into an alien land and a pagan culture,
    and endure the mocking taunts of strangers.

To THEM, who felt that everything they worked for had come
crashing down,
  who felt there was nothing left, no FUTURE, and no HOPE,
  God said, **I know the plans I have for you...**

His plans were not the same as their plans.
  Because of their sins and their rebellious spirit, He had to
  correct them and re-direct them.

Stop and consider, hasn't God been doing that to you?
Hasn't He already changed some of your plans?

It wasn't long ago, Christa, that you were being wheeled
into a hospital room
  for tests that revealed malformed blood vessels in your brain.

  Do you remember the emotional shock wave it sent through you,
    and how it seemed to put a giant question mark
    behind all those plans you made?

Jeff, your plans have changed too.
  There came that sobering realization that
  the DCE program wasn't for you,
    and then the decision to drop out of Concordia and postpone
    your education
      so that you could work to support your marriage.

Now that future you planned together has some question marks.

God has ways of changing our plans rather forcefully!

210

Even this week came another surprise –
the problem with your car and that big repair bill.

Not something you planned,
but it had to be fixed and paid for,
and it threw a wrench into your carefully planned budget
before you even moved to the home on Junior Street.

Listen well to such events.
They are a reminder that you are not in control of things.

God made you.
That means He has His own plans for you.

I don't mean to frighten you.
And I hope you won't enter marriage looking over your shoulder
wondering what God is going to do to you next, because
GOD'S PLANS FOR YOU ARE GOOD.

He said so.
I know the plans I have for you, plans for GOOD and not for EVIL,
to give you a future and a hope.

Lots of people think the will of God is a mysterious, and
Probably frightening thing.
But there is nothing mysterious about the heart of that will.

Jesus spoke it plainly:
I am come that you may have life,
and have it more abundantly.

God tipped His hand to each of you the day you were baptized.

He wanted to make each of you His own dear child,
to redeem you from your sins
and give you everlasting life instead of death.

Since you were little children,
  we parents have told you in every way we could
  about Jesus the Savior who came to enact that will and plan.

  Today I tell you again.
    Jesus loves you. Died for you. Rose to life for you.

  Everything else in your lives – and in the marriage you begin
  today – should serve that one great purpose:
    that you KNOW HIM and His saving power,
    and that you STAY CLOSE TO HIM by faith
      through all your lives.

That leads to one last point.

If God chooses to change your plans, you can be sure
  HE HAS A LOVING PURPOSE IN IT.
  Let me suggest at least one of those purposes.

  If things don't go as you hoped,
  you'll have to consider the possibility that God is
      STRIPPING AWAY YOUR PRIDE.

  For isn't it true that some of your desire
  to have things 'planned out'
    is really a desire to be in control?

  But then how would you learn SUBMISSION?
    How would you cultivate HUMILITY?
      How would you ever learn to TRUST God
      if He did not take the steering wheel out of your hands?

  You both discovered that in this past year,
    as you face trying times with health and with school issues.

    Those times brought you to your knees before your Father.

Wasn't it precisely there, at the end of <u>your</u> strength
that you found <u>His</u>?

I know the plans I have for you, says the Lord.

A humbling verse. An encouraging verse.

Ponder it well as you begin life together.

For I am not the only one who sees you with a father's eyes today.

God does too.
And He has plans for you.

IS THAT GOD CALLING?
Lamentations 3:22-40

You're watching your favorite TV show
or right in the middle of a meal
    when suddenly, unexpectedly, the phone rings!

    Loud. Insistent. Demanding immediate attention.

This morning's sermon is about PAIN.

Pain reminds me of that ringing phone.
    It is no respecter of persons, or of schedules!
    Whether it is a toothache or a tornado,
        pain jangles our nerves and won't let us go until
        we give it our attention.

A ringing phone brings a MESSAGE. So does PAIN.

    Over the years, I have watched people in the grip of an illness or grief,
        people in hospital beds and funeral homes,
        seeking the MESSAGE in what's happening to them.

        "What's the point of this suffering?" they ask.
        "What's this for?"

        HAS GOD HAD A HAND IN THIS?   IS THIS GOD CALLING?

That's a proper question
    that deserves an answer from the proper place.

Today we look together at one of the Bible's least-known and least-used books, the Book of Lamentations.

A lament is a cry of pain or sorrow.
The man who wrote this book knew about pain firsthand.

Jeremiah, haunted by the call of God, had done his best to obey it.

For years he preached it in every way he knew how.
    "REPENT! RETURN TO GOD!"

He screamed his warnings of doom to passers-by,
                wrote urgent letters to the king,
        acted out the Word of God in thought-provoking
        visual performances.

But his preaching was ignored.

Some of his listeners had turned on him, cursed him, and even
plotted against his life.

Now the worst had happened.

He had watched his terrifying prophecies
come true before his very eyes.

Jerusalem had fallen.
    During its two-year siege, Jeremiah watched emaciated
children wither away.
        He saw families cannibalize their own dead.

When the Babylonians burst through the city's defenses,
Jeremiah saw priests slaughtered in the Temple,
        women raped in the streets,
        and the city finally burned to the ground.

Centuries later, Michelangelo painted Jeremiah
on the ceiling of the Sistine Chapel as a lonely, brooding figure.

Jeremiah is often called 'The Weeping Prophet.'

216

The Book of Lamentations echoes with his gut-wrenching grief:

Chapter 1   **How lonely sits the city that was full of people! How like a widow she has become!**

Chapter 2   **The Lord has destroyed without mercy all the inhabitants of Jacob**

Chapter 3   **I am the man who has seen affliction under the rod of his wrath!**

In the center of this pain-filled book, Jeremiah wrestled with the meaning of it all,
> and in so doing he leaves a MESSAGE for those in every age who gasp with pain in their suffering.

Our text begins at verse 19:

READ VERSES 19-33, 37-40

The first lesson Jeremiah impresses on us is that when Pain's 'telephone' rings,
> it may be GOD CALLING!

In the tragedy of Jerusalem's fall,
it was not the Babylonian army, but GOD who was the subject.
> **He brings grief... who can speak and have it happen
> if the Lord has not decreed it?
> Is it not from the mouth of the Most High
> that both calamities and good things come?**

God BRINGS GRIEF, says Jeremiah in verse 32. Not WILLINGLY, NO!
> Yet He will afflict us if there is NEED.

In his book *THE PROBLEM OF PAIN,* C. S. Lewis says the same.
*God whispers to us in our pleasures, speaks in our conscience,
but shouts in our pains. It is his megaphone to rouse a deaf world.*

For some of us, I'm sure, this is a shocking, almost repulsive thought!
GOD – THE CAUSE OF PAIN? IT CANNOT BE!

The pastor of a church that had been heavily damaged in a tornado
tried to comfort his flock by saying,
"Whatever the cause of this storm, you can be sure that
God did not send it!"

He meant well, certainly. But was he speaking the truth?

Could he be so certain that God was NOT calling
through that destruction?

We have all been weaned on the verse that says **GOD IS LOVE**.
But we have trivialized love into a mere doting kindness
that would not, under any circumstances,
cause pain to its beloved.

We've transformed God into a slightly senile grandfather,
sitting in a porch swing
while his grandsons terrorize the neighborhood,
then saying of those rude little boys,
"What does it matter, so long as they are contented?"

Those who have known REAL LOVE know better!

A grandfather, or a father, a lover or a true friend
will not stand idly by and watch the ruin of someone he loves.

Real love intervenes.
Real love may rebuke, or correct, or even punish –
that is to say, real love will sometimes administer PAIN
if through pain help and healing may come.

Here in Lamentations the prophet says,
"Listen! In your very pains, God is calling you!"

Very well, then, we may ask, what is He trying to say to ME?

The second lesson in this text
   is that pain often brings God's CALL TO REPENT.

   The warfare Judah had just experienced, said Jeremiah,
   was a message about God's wrath against their sins.
      Jerusalem sinned grievously...
      why should any living man complain when punished for
         his sins?

When all is going well,
   Who among us would grieve over his sin?

   But pain pulls us up short.
   It interrupts our routine and makes us THINK.

   Lewis adds the observation, *Pain plants God's flag within the*
      rebel soul and summons us to repent of our sin.

We should always look for that purpose at work in God's WRATH.

   In the children's book *The Horse and His Boy*
      two runaway children named Shasta and Aravis, along with their
      horses, are pursued by wild lions as they run away from their
      homes.
         Aravis is even mauled.

   Later, Shasta meets the great King of Narnia, a talking Lion named
   Aslan. He is surprised to hear this good and gracious Lion say,
      There were no wild lions. I was the one who pursued you.
      It was I who wounded Aravis with my claws.

      Only then does Aslan explain the purpose of their pains and the
         correction He intended to humble their pride.

Is it not possible, then, when pain strikes,

when hijackers commandeer a plane,
   when cancer is diagnosed,
      when wild fires, auto accidents, and epidemics happen,

      that God Himself, the great Lion of the Tribe of Judah,
      has wounded us
         in order to humble us and bring us to repentance?

Our stubbornness will deny it.

   One day after visiting a woman with cancer, I spoke in the hallway
   with a family member, who told me bitterly,
      "She doesn't deserve any of this!"

   Can we safely say that of anyone? Or of ourselves?
      Is there NOTHING in us that needs attention and correction?
      Is there no SIN for which we need to repent?

   If that phone of yours is ringing, says Jeremiah,
      "Listen! That may be GOD calling to you!"

      Let us test and examine our ways and let us return to the Lord!

There is a third message here in Lamentations.
   Pain calls us to HOPE IN GOD.

   Those last two words – IN GOD – need underlining.
      For we are always pinning our hopes somewhere else -
      our health, our children, our investments.

      We lay up treasures on earth.
      Meanwhile, we take a scissors and clip off eternity.

   Pain may be the only thing that can waken us to the truth that
      ALL ELSE WILL FAIL EXCEPT GOD.

      If we hope at all, it must be anchored in Him.

There was one man who hoped that way – our Lord Jesus Christ.
Jesus Christ knew pain... better than Jeremiah did,
better than we do!

When He met pain, He put his hope in God alone.
How perfectly the words of Lamentations describe Him:
He **waited quietly.**
He **sat alone in silence.**
He **gave his cheek to the smiters.**

When at last He died, the promise spoken by Jeremiah in this text
came true:
The Lord will not cast (him) off forever.

The third day He rose again... and BEHOLD!
His pain became our redemption.
His death became our Life!

So God, through Christ, transforms even our most frightful
BURDENS into BLESSINGS.

There's an old legend that long ago,
birds were thin, sleek creatures who lived entirely on the
ground.
Being slim as they were, they could run very fast.

One day God gathered them all together and affixed to their
backs a heavy load.
The birds protested bitterly, for so heavy were these loads,
the poor birds could no longer run, but now only hop.

As the days passed, while the other birds cried, one bird was
busy wondering at God's purpose.
By experimenting, he found that his burden could, with
effort, be maneuvered back and forth.

It wasn't long until, behold, he FLEW!

For as you have guessed, those burdens were what we now call WINGS.

HOPE IN GOD, my friend!

If he has given you a painful burden, some SUFFERING to carry, pray to Him and trust His purpose.

If He does not remove it,
    it may be that He plans for it to be your WINGS,
    a load that will finally LIFT you CLOSER TO HIM.

Is God calling you through some load of pain?

Take time to LISTEN.
Examine your heart and repent.

Place your full HOPE in Jesus the Savior.
He will turn your LAMENTATION into THANKSGIVING.

His grace will teach you to sing this song:
    The steadfast love of the Lord never ceases.
    His mercies never come to an end.
    They are new every morning.
    GREAT is thy faithfulness.

GOD PLANTED A TREE
Ezekiel 17:22-24

_____

Here in the Pacific Northwest, we have some of the world's most
beautiful trees.
   Hemlock and Spruce,
      Douglas Fir, Giant Sequoia,
         Western Red Cedar, Ponderosa Pine,
         and more...

Loggers look to them for their livelihood.
   Environmentalists see them as a dwindling treasure to be
   protected, along with the spotted owls and other endangered
   creatures that live there.
      Vacationers like me simply stand underneath them and look
      up in awe!

TREES are everywhere in Scripture too.

   The Tree of Knowledge in the Garden of Eden,
      and the Tree of Life in Heaven, with its 12 kinds of fruit.

   The oaks of Mamre where the patriarchs renewed their covenant,
      and the olive grove in Gethsemane where Jesus prayed.

   The low-hanging tree where Absalom was caught by his hair,
      and the towering tree in Nebuchadnezzar's dream.

There are trees in stories, trees in parables, trees in the Psalms.

And why not?
   Israel was a dry land that needed shade.
      Israel was a hungry land that needed fruit – figs and olives
      and dates.

It is not surprising
   that when God's messengers wanted to speak His Word
   in a way that people understood,
      they would often use 'tree talk.'

This morning's Old Testament lesson from Ezekiel is one of those.

Open your ears for some tree talk:

READ THE TEXT

There was a good reason for Ezekiel's message. He was sent to a
nation in despair.
   Their glory was gone. Their hopes crushed.

   Jerusalem had fallen to the Babylonians!
      The temple was burned.
         King Zedekiah was slain.
            Thousands were taken into exile.

To a nation in ruin, at a time of bleak despair, the prophet announces
hope this way:
   GOD WILL PLANT A TREE!

   Among the ashes and the tears, there will grow up A TREE!

Listen carefully to the prophet's description of what this tree will be:
   A SMALL TREE
      A MOUNTAIN TREE
         A CEDAR TREE
            A BLESSING TREE
               A WISDOM TREE.

   Listen well. The prophet speaks also to us.

First, he says, it will be a SMALL TREE.   **A shoot...a tender sprig.**

224

An insignificant-looking <u>beginning</u> … that will lead to a great <u>ending</u>. That's what happened in the aftermath of the Mt. St. Helens eruption.

If you toured the site during those first years after that fateful day, you remember that the landscape was barren, almost lunar in its desolation.

Four billion board feet of timber on 230 square miles had been blown over - incinerated!

Barren slopes were covered with ash.

But just a few years later, there they were.
Tiny shoots. Tender sprigs.

Sprouting out of the desolation like flags of hope to announce, "A forest will grow here again!"

Today, years later, there are trees twenty, even thirty feet tall nourished by the ashes.

The animals again have a home.

The promise of life renewed is coming true.

They started small, but those trees are growing bigger year by year!

Second, he says, this tree will be planted on a MOUNTAIN.

Here in the Northwest, that's the place to go if you want to see great trees.

Head to the Mt. Hood forest, or the Coast range.

Mt. Rainier or Crater Lake.

But the prophet has another mountain in mind:

On the mountain heights of Israel I will plant it.

The mountain in the prophet's mind is small in size, but great in significance.

The mountain where stood the temple. Mt. Zion.

That mountain, which Isaiah promises (2:2)
> **will be established as chief among the mountains...**
> **and raised above the hills, and all nations will**
> **stream to it.**

Got it so far? A SMALL tree.... planted on Mt. Zion.

What kind of tree?
That's point number three:
God will **take a shoot from the top of a CEDAR.**

Why a cedar?
Why not an olive, or a palm tree, a fig or a sycamore?

Because the cedar is a kingly sort of tree.
It's the tree kings used when they built
their palaces and temples.

Cedars of Lebanon were the trees King Solomon bought from
Hiram of Tyre
and floated on rafts down the coast
to build his magnificent Temple in Jerusalem.

Cedars of Lebanon.   So kings themselves were called!

The king of Assyria, says Ezekiel in chapter 31, was a cedar of
Lebanon.
King Jehoash boasted in 2 Kings 14, **I am a cedar of Lebanon.**
His enemy was dismissed as a mere thistle!

The hope is taking a particular shape.
This little tree, planted on a mountain, is to be a KINGLY tree.

There's more.
Ezekiel's fourth point: It will be full of BLESSING.

226

It will produce branches and bear FRUIT...birds...
will find shelter in the shade of its branches.

FRUIT AND SHADE are two things we want
in the trees we plant today.

When Sue and I moved to our home in Oregon City, we planted
fruit trees at the corners of the back yard.
How we've enjoyed the apples and the Italian prunes!

The apple tree, now grown large, has provided an additional gift
of shade from the hot summer sun.
We sit beneath it, shielded from the heat, reading or napping.

That blessing is not just for us!
The birds find it too.
This year we've added a small bird house
and a hummingbird feeder.

Finally, says Ezekiel, this tree of BLESSING
will also become a learning tree, dispensing God's WISDOM.

All the trees of the field will know that I, the Lord,
bring down the tall tree and make the low tree grow tall.
I dry up the green tree and make the dry tree flourish.

One tree teaching other trees twin lessons
about how God deals with us.

The first is a lesson about JUDGMENT:
The high and mighty humbled – like the trees blown down
at Mt. St. Helens.
The self-sufficient squeezed dry.

The second a message of HOPE,
anchored in the providence of God –

227

in His freedom to take things small and make them great,
to take things dry and dead and make them fruitful again.

All of this in a TREE that God will plant, Ezekiel told them.

We today can use this hope-filled picture, because we live as a nation in ruin,
in a time of bleak despair for many people.

Jobs lost. Businesses closed. General Motors bankrupt!
Homes foreclosed. People living in tent cities.
Budgets cut to the bone. School teachers laid off.

We live, as it were, in a kind of Mount St. Helens blast zone,
blown away by all that has happened. As a result,
our marriages are distressed,
our minds and hearts are depressed, and
our congregation and school are experiencing unrest.

This word of Ezekiel is appointed not only for this Sunday, but for this time.

Hear it again, child, further, deeper. Spoken to your soul…and mine.
GOD PLANTED A TREE!

PLANTED, He said. Past tense. An accomplished fact.
Come with me. I'll show you.

A **small tree?** Yes, it was, at first.
Put on your Isaiah 53 glasses and have a closer look:
He grew up like a tender shoot, and like a root out of dry ground.

This tiny tree, this man-child, planted in a manger in Bethlehem.
JESUS IS HIS NAME.

228

Tiny he began, but tiny he did <u>not</u> remain!

He made his way to the **mountains**, where trees grow.
The mount where he preached.
The mount of his transfiguration.
Mount Zion too, just as Ezekiel said.

There on Zion in the temple of Solomon, there in the cedar halls,
he listened as a 12-year-old boy,
and taught as a 30-year-old man.

There finally He was firmly planted,
pinned to a cross-shaped tree, watered by tears and blood.
GOD PLANTED A TREE ON CALVARY.

His enemies did not recognize the wood of this tree,
but you know what kind he was:
a CEDAR OF LEBANON – a KINGLY TREE –
so read the sign above his head:
Jesus of Nazareth, the king of the Jews

From that kingly Cedar Tree, planted on Mt. Zion,
have come the BLESSINGS we so desperately need –
FRUIT AND SHADE.

We who live in a dry and hungry land
find in Him abundant FRUIT that feeds, strengthens, and
refreshes us.

A few years ago I preached a funeral sermon for a woman who
knew Jesus intimately, and savored the fruits of His saving work.

On a table in front, I placed canning jars she had filled
with peaches, pears, apples and prunes.

But the real fruit was what He had produced in her life –
love, joy, peace, patience, and all the rest.

Have you eaten of these lately?
Fed some to your hungry neighbor?
    Taste and see the fruit of this tree.

Rest beneath His SHADE.
    We who are beaten down by the heat of personal hurts,
    withered and dried
    and almost dead because of our failures and fears,
        find in Him a blessed, cooling SHADE,
            rest for our tired hearts and crumbled hopes,
                forgiveness when our relationships are ruined
                and our bridges burned.

Knowing Jesus is like coming out of the HOT SUN
into the lovely SHADE of a great tree.

    "I have never known such peace as I have found just lately,"
    said a woman to me years ago.

        She had just finished an instruction class.

        There she had heard for the first time the sure word of pardon
            spoken over a life of failure.

A BLESSING TREE He is, with fruit and shade.
And yes, a WISDOM TREE too!

Sit under this WISDOM TREE
    and learn from Him how God deals with us.

    For we also are trees in God's field.
        Gathered round Him, we learn from Jesus about
        JUDGMENT AND HOPE

The Judgment that comes to humble our pride.

That word has come to me again and again through the years
on the lips of His people –
   like my college roommate in Michigan
   who showed me my pride
      and a dear older woman in Ohio who rebuked my
      slanderous tongue.

Words that showed me my sin and called me to my knees.

Jesus is our WISDOM TREE.

   HIS words of Judgment are paired with words of genuine HOPE.
   Words that take us from the depths and lift us up high.
   Words I have also heard you speak to me on His behalf –
      words in which you say you see Him working in our midst,
      words of encouragement to try again.

We are seated here as if in a great forest, watered abundantly,
growing year by year.

In the center that great TREE God planted.
   And all around Him, we ourselves growing tall and strong.
   Growing to be just like Him, the Tree God planted.

   Evie Tornquist sang it in these words:

      I saw a tree by the riverside one day as I walked along.
      Straight as an arrow and pointing to the sky growing tall and
         strong.
      "How do you grow so tall and strong?"
         I said to the riverside tree.
      This is the song my tree friend sang to me:
         I've got roots growing down to the water,
         I've got leaves growing up to the sunshine,
            and the fruit that I bear is a sign of the life in me.
         I am shade from the hot summer sundown.
         I am nest for the birds of the heavens.

I'm becoming what the Lord of trees has meant me to be:
a strong young tree.

Take heart! Find hope in the prophet's proclamation today:
GOD PLANTED A TREE.

THEY DARED TO BE DIFFERENT
Daniel 3

Sit back in your seat, now, child,
 and I will tell you a story about three young men, who showed
 courage in the face of great danger –
  three young men who DARED TO BE DIFFERENT.

Long ago and far away in a land called Babylon,
 King Nebuchadnezzar made a gigantic golden idol
 90 feet tall and ten feet wide.

 He set it up in the Plain of Dura
 and called all his advisers and officials together
  for the dedication of that image.

 Everyone came as commanded.
 They stood before the image of gold.

  Then the king's messenger proclaimed: **This is what you must
   do! As soon as you hear the sound of music, you must FALL
   DOWN AND WORSHIP the king's golden image. Whoever
   disobeys will be thrown immediately into a BURNING,
   FIERY FURNACE!**

 The music began to play,
 and everyone fell down and worshipped the image.

  Well, not quite everyone!
  Some officials raced to where the king was sitting and said,
   "O KING! You commanded <u>everyone</u> to worship the image
   when the music began. But there are three young men
   among your officials – 3 Jews! – Shadrach, Meshach, and
   Abednego – who are paying no attention to your command.

They won't serve your god!
They won't worship your golden image!"

Furious with rage, the king summoned Shadrach, Meshach, and
Abednego. They were brought before the king.
   He said, "Is it true that you will not serve my gods or bow down
   to my image?
      Well, then, I will give you one more chance!
      When you hear the music, bow down!
      If you won't, then into the FIERY FURNACE you will go,
         and then what god is there who can rescue you?"

Shadrach, Meshach and Abednego stood their ground.
   "O Nebuchadnezzar, we do not need to defend ourselves.
   If you throw us into the furnace, our God will save us
   from your hand.
      BUT EVEN IF HE DOES NOT, we want you to
      know, O King, that we will NOT serve your gods
         or bow down to your image."

That did it! Nebuchadnezzar blew his top!
   He ordered his men to heat that furnace 7 times hotter.

   He shouted at his soldiers to tie up Shadrach, Meshach, and
   Abednego, and throw them into the fiery furnace.

The soldiers obeyed. The furnace was so hot
that the soldiers died as they threw the three young men into it!

Then King Nebuchadnezzar leaped to his feet in amazement.
   "Weren't there three young men thrown into the furnace?
   But LOOK! Now I see four men walking around unbound and
   unharmed...and the fourth looks like a son of the gods!"

He went closer and summoned the three to come out.
   Everyone crowded around them, and all could see that the fire
   had not touched them, and there was not even

234

a smell of smoke on them!

Nebuchadnezzar said,
"Praise be to the God of Shadrach, Meshach and Abednego,
who rescued his servants! They were willing to risk their lives
rather than worship any god except their own.
Let no one speak against this God, for
no other God can save people this way."

Then Shadrach, Meshach and Abednego were promoted to more
honored posts.

This story, so beloved to children, is much more than a children's
story.
It is a story all of us adults would do well to hear,
because what they faced, we face!

They faced a COMMAND TO CONFORM.
Before them stood a golden statue nine stories tall.
The words of the king's messenger were unmistakable:
"When you hear the music,
DO WHAT OTHERS ARE DOING
AND SAY WHAT THEY ARE SAYING!"

There are no golden statues
at the Abernethy Center or Pioneer Courthouse Square,
but there don't need to be!

For we are surrounded by images more sophisticated
and far more seductive than any golden statue...

Bank towers, Bunny ears, and the Golden Arches,
the horns of the Dodge Ram,
the sculpted face of the Marlboro Man,
and the America's plastic Trinity:
VISA, MasterCard, and American Express.

The music plays and we are summoned to bow down and take part
in the devotional rites of our dominant culture,
   which (in case you haven't noticed) take place not in churches,
   but in shopping malls, sports stadiums, casinos and cyberspace.

   So have another drink and play along, won't you?

The horns and flutes that King Nebuchadnezzar trotted out have been
replaced
   by MTV, Madison Avenue jingles, and synthesizers,
   but the message is the same:

   "Do what others are doing, and say what others are saying"

The CULTURE calls us to a kind of worship of stuff and self.
   It sings into our ears a litany of instant gratification:
   "Wouldn't you really rather have…"
      "You deserve a break today…"

   and yes, "When you want the car, you want the car!"

It assumes, and wants you to assume, that everyone's Number One
priority
   is to acquire as much money and stuff as possible,
   as fast as possible.

It preaches a Gospel of RELATIVISM that affirms no certain right and
wrong,
   no truth except 'what's true for you.'

   Almost every student entering the university today believes,
   or says he believes, that truth is relative,
      says Doctor Allen Bloom in his disturbing book
      THE CLOSING OF THE AMERICAN MIND.

Shadrach, Meshach and Abednego were faced with the summons to
conform as they stood on the Plain of Dura.

236

But you and I don't even need to leave home,
   for the seductive music plays nightly on our TV sets
   and is a mouse click away on our computers.

   The message that comes electronically and digitally is the
   same old song that was playing back in Babylon:
      "When you hear the music,
      DO WHAT WE ARE DOING, SAY WHAT WE ARE SAYING!"

But Shadrach, Meshach and Abednego said, "NO!"

While others were bowing down, they stood unbending.
While others babbled, they held a determined SILENCE.

Like Mahatma Gandhi standing up to the might of the British in
India
   and Martin Luther facing down Emperor Charles V at Worms,
   they DARED TO BE DIFFERENT.

   They dared to disobey the king's command
      in order to show homage to a Higher Lord and be faithful
      to His Truth.

That act took COURAGE!
   The king's power to harm them was real.
   That furnace was NO MIRAGE!

In a fallen world, the decision to OBEY GOD will always lead to
suffering.
   If you decide to stand up to the kids on the playground
      or the people at your office,
      you can expect to face a 'fiery ordeal.'

We Christians in the 21st century could learn something
from these three brave young men.

   First, ACTIONS SPEAK LOUDER THAN WORDS.

Talk is cheap, and a lot of Christians today are filling broadcasts
and blogs with militant rhetoric,
    when what is needed (desperately!) is that we live
    lives that are different, lives marked by plain goodness
    and simple OBEDIENCE TO GOD:
                telling the truth
                staying sexually pure
        and loving people more than we love money.

DEEDS lend substance to CREEDS.

St. Francis said:
    Preach the Gospel all the time. If necessary, use words!

Shadrach, Meshach and Abednego ACTED OUT their confession
of faith.
    That action opened the door to speaking to the king, who
    wanted to know what made them tick.

Let your ACTIONS speak first.
Then people will listen to your words.

Second, OBEDIENCE TO GOD INCLUDES NO GUARANTEE
            OF PERSONAL SAFETY.

    Did you hear what the three young men said?
        **God will save us…but even if NOT, we…will not
        worship your image.**

    Even if God would <u>not</u> come to their rescue!

    Centuries later, Martin Luther said something similar:
        *Even if there were more devils at Worms than tiles on the
        rooftops, I would still go and face the Emperor.*

    Are we so willing as they to OBEY GOD
    with no guarantee that He will shield us?

Shadrach, Meshach and Abednego DARED TO BE DIFFERENT.
And when they did, they found they did not stand ALONE.

There with them, in the center of that furnace, was
one like a son of the gods.

That is the THIRD great truth we learn from these three young men.
THOSE WHO OBEY GOD WILL NOT STAND ALONE.

The good news I share with you is that
Jesus Christ, the Son of God
has come to STAND WITH YOU in your need...

I AM WITH YOU... WITH YOU ALWAYS is His sure promise.

He offers no guarantees that we will not endure a fiery ordeal,
but he promises we SHALL NOT BE ALONE.

That's why Jesus came.

To be with sinners in their hour of need.
To call us to turn from sin to something better.
To free us to be
DIFFERENT than we were
DIFFERENT from the world around us.

We may DARE TO BE DIFFERENT because we ARE different.
Through the mercy of Jesus, we are different persons,
NEW CREATURES ENTIRELY.

Then when our fiery furnace comes,
when Satan accuses us and our guilty conscience burns like fire
or when other people turn up the heat and our fears flame high,

JESUS COMES TO TAKE HIS STAND WITH US
to forgive the sin
and set our hearts at peace.

It was the presence of Jesus that sustained Polish priest Maximilian Kolbe
    as he descended with nine other prisoners into
    Isolation Barracks 11 at Auschwitz.

    Condemned to death with those men,
        he shared with them in words and songs
        the very presence of Christ.

    The guards who came to finish the prisoners off
    remembered his face — a saintly face with the smile of an angel —
        as if the Son of God stood by him.

Shadrach, Meshach and Abednego DARED TO BE DIFFERENT,
    and because they did, they MADE A DIFFERENCE.

    The king changed his mind, gave praise to God, and even changed the law!

It has always been so.
    Nothing done for the Lord's sake, no matter how small,
    goes to waste.

    Maximilian Kolbe touched the hearts of his Nazi guards.
        Martin Luther changed the spiritual map of Europe.
            The smallest act of love in the name of Jesus is
            a powerful seed
                that brings a harvest.

It happened years ago in Thailand.

A young Buddhist boy from a poor village was awarded
a Fulbright scholarship.
    Off he went to Prince Royal College, a school in Chingmei
    sponsored by a Christian church.
        There, for the first time in his life, he had enough to eat.

One night a few weeks after his arrival,
his classmates found him crying.
When they asked why, he told them it was because he had
enough to eat while his family back home did not.

The new friends, all Christians, decided they must do something.
The next day, though they themselves were poor, they pooled
their money and bought a sack of rice, which they sent to the
boy's family.

He was dumbfounded that these new friends would care that much
for a family they had never met.
Never had he experienced such care.
It was new to him – completely DIFFERENT.

So moved was he that he decided to study about their faith.
He became a Christian.
Today he is the director of the Christian Student Center
in Bangkok.

All because those boys dared to be DIFFERENT, and show love in
an unexpected, sacrificial way.

It will happen through you, too!

For all of you that trust in Jesus Christ ARE filled with a different spirit.

When culture's music plays, don't bow down!
Instead, stand up for Jesus.

You will discover that He has come to stand with you.

A FEW GOOD MEN AND WOMEN
Amos 5:12-15

READ THE TEXT

They are looking, they say, for 'a few good men.'

They are Marine recruiters, and they mean what they say.
   If you want to be a Marine, you'd better be GOOD –
      in good physical shape
        good with a weapon
          good at taking orders.

  For the job is a tough one. Marines are front-line fighters, ready
   and willing to die in the service of their country.

  People who are that good are FEW.
    Not many want such a job.
    And of those who want it, not many will be able to handle it.

    "Could it be YOU?" they ask.
    "Could you be one of the FEW… the PROUD… the MARINES?"

I am a recruiter too. For God's army.
   If you want to sign on, you will have to be GOOD.   Very good!

  The job to which I am calling you is a tough one –
  far tougher than being a Marine!

    The tour of duty is not for a few years, but for LIFE.
      The fight is against an enemy that cannot be killed with
      bullets.
        There will be no parades in your honor.
          And no pay….although I have it on good authority
          that there will be a significant reward after you die.

243

This morning, I am looking for a few good men...and women.
   Children too!

When it comes to serving in God's army,
most of us like to think we are GOOD ENOUGH...
   nice folks who wouldn't hurt a fly
      taxpayers
         hard-working students
            honest citizens.

"We're good enough!" we say.

Oh, we admit to a few bad habits, but nothing to be alarmed about.
   My sister-in-law once summed it up in words I have often heard:
   "People," she told me brightly, "are basically good!"

Good enough, at least, that God should be happy to employ us just as
we are.

   Read the Bible?   Pray?   Go to church?   Witness to others?
      Well and good, if you choose to do that sort of thing,
      but not really necessary because we are GOOD ENOUGH.

It is a lie!   A piece of propaganda from the Enemy himself.

   Those who believe they are good enough for God's service just as
   they are
      remind me of a paunchy 50-year-old who thinks he can
      set aside his can of Budweiser,
         jump up from his couch,
            and hit a home run in a World Series game!

For all of us who think we are GOOD – or at least 'good enough' –
   this Bible text has a lesson as sobering as a slap in the face:
      the GOOD are very few,
      and you and I are <u>not</u> among them!

Who says so?

God does!   It is He who says,
  **I know how many are your transgressions, and how great
  are your sins.**

  God knows. He records our deeds more thoroughly, more
  accurately than those surveillance cameras
  that scan us wherever we go.

  Those cameras, by the way, are making a difference in our courts.
    Defendants who stubbornly assert their innocence
    grow strangely quiet when confronted by videotapes of their
      words and deeds.

    Years ago already, Marion Berry, the mayor of Washington, DC,
    was shown a videotape of an illicit drug deal he had made.
      After he saw the tape, his protests of innocence ceased,
      and he was quickly convicted.

How would we do, brothers and sisters, if God were to replay
  the previously-hidden parts of our lives here in front of church
  on the big screen?

  I can tell you what the verdict would be:
    There is none that does good, the Bible says in Romans 3,
    No, not one!

  Will you admit that with me this morning?

If the Bible is telling us the truth –
  if the 'GOOD' are that few, and sin is that prevalent,
  then we must all go back to the very BEGINNING.

If we are to serve in God's Army, we must go to BOOT CAMP
  where we get his basic training.

BASIC TRAINING in God's boot camp begins with silence.
He who is prudent will keep silent in such a time,
for it is an evil time.

KEEP SILENT.

A few years ago, someone gave me a book for Christmas - a book by
Mother Teresa called *A SIMPLE PATH*.

Can you guess where Mother Teresa says the path begins?
With SILENCE...

Some of God's greatest soldiers – Moses, Elijah, and St. Paul –
began their basic training in the desert,
a place of immense and utter silence.

The SILENCE to which God calls us, however, is not an EMPTY silence.
Rather, it is a WAITING silence that listens for a Word from God,
then a REFLECTIVE silence that ponders the message
in that word,
and finally a REPENTANT silence that stills its proud clamoring
with a simple prayer, "Father, forgive me."

I am going to ask you to do that now as a part of this sermon.
For the next interval of time, we will all be quiet – me too!

Imagine that we have just arrived at God's boot camp.
We green recruits are sitting here together.

I invite you to look up at the screen, and ponder the QUESTIONS
that will appear there.
Let's be SILENT a while and let God address our hearts:

(project on screen)
Have I neglected PRAYER and the WORD?

Have I met my NEIGHBORS and listened to them?

Have I valued MONEY more than SERVICE?

Have I wounded someone with my TONGUE?

Have I made SPEAKING about Jesus my greatest priority?

Much can happen in our SILENCE. That's where God has us begin.
But He does not leave us there. Silence is only the beginning.

The fruit of silence, says mother Teresa, *is prayer. The fruit of
prayer is FAITH.*

The faith to which the Bible calls us
is <u>not</u> a faith in ourselves, but rather a faith in God, in His promises,
and especially in His grace.

It may be, said the prophet Amos, **that the Lord will be GRACIOUS.**

That's how GOODNESS comes. By GRACE.
By grace are you saved through faith is how the Bible says it.

One of our contemporary songs says it this way:
*Only by grace can we enter
Only by grace can we stand
Not by our human endeavor
But by the blood of the Lamb...*

God wants a few GOOD men and women.
Men and women who know that their goodness is not a WORK,
but a GIFT.

Years ago, a missionary sat with a Native American man on a
reservation in Oklahoma. Patiently the missionary had explained
the story of Jesus and the meaning of grace, and he asked if the
man understood.

That man said, very simply:

"He pay, or I pay. HE PAY, so I NO PAY!"

When it comes to GOODNESS, the truth is, there was only one man who was
   'good enough' as he was.

   That man was Jesus, the sinless Son of God.

   HE PAID!
     His was the expense of keeping the Law perfectly. His was the
      expense of shedding blood to pay the penalty for sin.

     Ours was the blessing, the benefit...
      and His goodness becomes ours when we trust in Him
      as Savior.

Have you? If you have not, will you?

For is you will, there is something great and good God has for you to do.
   The TASK to which I would recruit you this morning
   is not simply to BE GOOD!

     God does not want you simply to sit in church an hour a week
     and soak up some grace, belch a pious belch, and go home
     fat and satisfied!

People who do that and nothing more are GOOD FOR NOTHING!

When a Marine finished Basic Training,
   he is not sent home with a medal for good training!

     He is sent on to some post, some station, some assignment
     where his work <u>really</u> begins!

Through Jesus, God has made us GOOD FOR SOMETHING.

What is that 'something'?

Amos tells us,
> **Seek good, and not evil. Hate evil and love good, and establish justice in the gate.**

The GATE was not the gate of the Temple.
It was the gate of the city.
    The place in every town where deals were struck,
        decisions were made,
      and just verdicts rendered.

    The GATE -- That's where you go to work each day.
        It's where you do business with your customers,
      eat lunch with fellow students,
      meet your neighbor and listen to him.

    The GATE is where someone is waiting for your decision,
      counting on you for help,
      watching to see if you'll set an example.

    It's where you'll be going when you leave church today,
    where it will soon be obvious whether your Christian faith
      is just a lot of pious talk
      or really means something.

In one of his books, George MacDonald tells of a businessman who sat in church and finally came to a real faith.
    That's when his churchgoing stopped being merely a comfortable habit and started being an arduous mission.

    "What am I to do with what I've heard?" he asked himself.
    "How much shall I charge my customers?
    "How often, and how fully, must I now begin to tell the truth?"

Good questions! The sort we must face if we are part of God's army.

Several years ago I sat in the Kingdome in Seattle
with 55,000 other men at a Promise Keepers gathering.
Like being part of a wonderful army it was!

All of us there were given a challenging mission:
as men who follow Jesus, our great Captain, what GOOD would
God have us do when we got home to our wives, our children,
our churches and our communities?

There it was!   Marching orders.
Orders all 55,000 of us were called to follow and obey every day
from then on.

Today, I am here to recruit you, and then to send you out on your
mission.

In truth it is not I, but GOD who is calling out to see
if there are a few good MEN...
and WOMEN...
and CHILDREN too
who are willing to say YES.

Not many these days want such a task.

But for all those who do, the grace of Jesus will be more than enough.

DOVE FLYING THE WRONG WAY
Jonah 1:1-3; 3:1-2

One of the tragedies of literature
is that most people know nothing about the Book of Jonah
except that in it, a man is swallowed by a great fish.

In actuality, this little book is one of the most significant prophetic
books in all literature.
One Bible student, who says he has read it at least 100 times,
admits that he cannot read it without his pulse beating faster
and tears coming to his eyes...

"It is," he says, "one of the deepest, grandest parts of the Bible."

Another writer calls it "a rock thrown through the window
of one's soul."

Jonah is a short book – only 4 chapters, just 48 verses in all.
But it is LONG in content – and very instructive, especially today.

It is a book to be read by us all.

So what's the message in it?
That people can survive being swallowed by whales?
That God can do miracles?

Well, yes! But far more.
This is a book that calls us to think as God thinks
about people who are very different from us...

for here we meet a prophet who mistakenly thinks that
God must endorse all his prejudices.

That's enough introduction.

Let's get to the text itself and meet this fellow Jonah head-on.
Please open your bulletins to the sermon.
You'll see that the text is printed out underneath:

READ VERSES 1-2

At this point, one might expect to hear the words, "and he arose and went."
Instead comes a surprise. Jonah heads the opposite direction!

READ VERSE 3

Jonah goes AWOL! He runs away!

If the name Jonah means 'Dove,' as most scholars think it does,
then this is a DOVE DETERMINED TO FLY THE WRONG WAY!

What was Jonah's problem, anyway?
What was it about God's instructions that made him feel he must stage this personal rebellion?

Was it too BIG an assignment?

Nineveh <u>was</u> a huge city for that time in history.
Archeologists have determined that it was about 8 miles in circumference, with several hundred thousand inhabitants.

Was it too FAR AWAY?

Nineveh was 600 miles east of Israel. That's a long way to go to preach a sermon!
But I hasten to add that Tarshish, where Jonah tried to flee, was nearly 5 times as far away!

Was the job TOO TOUGH?

After all, Nineveh did have a reputation

252

for wickedness and cruelty.
There was cultic prostitution at its temples,
and its army was known to have skinned its captives alive!

But NO. None of these things made Jonah run away.
The real reason is much stranger:
JONAH WAS AFRAID HE WOULD SUCCEED!

Jonah was a Jew.
The people of Nineveh were Assyrians – deadly enemies
of the Jews.

Jonah knew that God was MERCIFUL.

He feared that if he went and preached to the people of Nineveh,
and if they repented,
GOD MIGHT FORGIVE THEM!

He admits it to God later on in chapter 4:
**That is why I made haste to flee to Tarshish; for I knew
that you are a gracious God, and merciful!**

Jonah didn't want Nineveh forgiven!
He wanted it DAMNED!   Wiped off the face of the earth!

The way some of us feel about militant Muslim terrorists,
or the drug cartels in Mexico,
or child molesters.

Does it SHOCK YOU to hear a prophet of God take such a view?

It should, for this is NOT the Spirit of God!

God's attitude is the opposite of Jonah's.   We read it everywhere
in Scripture:
**God wants <u>all men</u> to be saved and to come to the knowledge
of the Truth.**

253

Make disciples of all nations
Be my witnesses... to the uttermost parts of the earth.

THAT is what God wants.

Do God's people share God's attitude?

William Carey, a shoemaker in Northampton, England,
had read about Captain Cook's voyages to Hawaii.

One day in 1786 he attended a meeting of ministers and said,
"It is the duty of Christians to attempt to spread the Gospel
among heathen nations."

A minister named Ryland sprang to his feet and thundered at Carey,
"YOUNG MAN, SIT DOWN! When God pleases to convert the
heathen, He will do it without your aid...or mine!"

Fortunately, Carey did not sit, but pressed on
until he had formed the London Mission Society.
Seven years later, he himself became a missionary to India.

Are we more like William Carey... or Pastor Ryland?

Do we share God's CONCERN FOR THE LOST?
If so, why don't more of us volunteer to go?

If we cannot go in person, how generously do we support OTHERS
to go in our place with our mission offerings?

Last year at Trinity, we sent $4800 to 'missions' of all kinds.
That's 7% of our budget, about $48 per person.
It would support a mission family of four overseas for two weeks.

But why limit ourselves to those who are FAR AWAY?

What about the lost here in our own little town?

254

There are 1400 people here that have no connection
to a Christian Church.

Jesus said, **YOU shall be my witnesses!**

I'm glad to say that we have a newly-elected Evangelism team.
But Jesus had more in mind!
  He did not say, "The Evangelism Team shall be my witnesses."
  He said, "YOU..."

  How many of us DO that? Speak about Jesus to others?

And if we are going to be HONEST with ourselves and God,
  mustn't we confess to sharing some of Jonah's prejudices?

  How much do we really care about Hispanic immigrants?
    or welfare recipients?
      or Jehovah's Witnesses?
        or gay rights activists?

  If there was a gathering of Neo-Nazis,
    and a tornado demolished the building where they were meeting
    and all of them were killed, how many of us would be thinking,
      "Serves them RIGHT! I'm glad God finally DID something!"

Stop and think.
  How often, as we express our dislike for certain groups of people,
  do we begin to sound uncomfortably like Jonah?

  If God dispatched us to go, to befriend, and to reach out to
    one of the groups we love to hate,
    would we pull a Jonah-act and become
        DOVES FLYING THE WRONG WAY TOO?

Do we really think we can escape from God?

Jonah thought so!

He boarded a ship in order to **flee from the presence of the Lord.**

Did he think God was some kind of tribal deity? Just the 'local sheriff' in Israel? Hadn't he read Psalm 139?
  Where can I flee from your presence?
  If I go up to the heavens, you are there.
  If I make my bed in the depths, you are there.
  If I settle on the far side of the sea, even there your hand
    will hold me fast!

You can't run away from God. He sees everything. Everyone!
  In the sky over our heads there are SPY SATELLITES
  with such sophisticated cameras
    that they can watch golfers on a green, and even see the ball!

God has far better vision. He sees all the way into our hearts!
  Those who try to RUN AWAY from His call, EVADE His mission,
  and AVOID the people to whom He sends us,
    will one day have to stand and face him.

  On Judgment Day there will be no ships to Tarshish.
  No place at all to hide.

Thankfully, God did not leave His wrong-way prophet alone.

He pursued Jonah with a storm,
  and even with a specially-appointed fish!

  For He is a loving and stubbornly persistent God – also with His own people when they persist in being stubborn and rebellious!

  He could shrug us off and say, "I'll get someone else for the job."

  But NO... He keeps after us.
    Sometimes He sends us "stormy weather" – an illness, an accident, or the loss of a job.

Sometimes it is a "storm on two legs" – a persistent pastor,
   a determined spouse or friend.

And don't we WANT that?

ANYTHING rather than to let us go to Tarshish and to hell!

But best of all is the news that God dispatched His Son
   to seek us out,
      to SAVE us,
         to TURN us around and head us in the RIGHT DIRECTION

Jesus became a latter-day Jonah
   sent by God on a mission of mercy
   to God's own deadly enemies – US!

   Jesus endured the worst storm,
   the darkness at noon that came as He hung on the cross.

   While we were yet sinners, wrote St. Paul,
      Jesus went down, not merely into a fish,
      but into the very jaws of death, of the grave, of hell itself
         to rescue and reclaim us.

No longer are we strangers and foreigners, but once again we are
   His very own people, cleansed and changed.
   Indeed, we are prophets charged to bring His message of life
   As Jonah was of old.

WHAT MERCY!

From the lips of that Savior comes a call, and then again,
   Follow me!   Be my witnesses!

   A SECOND CHANCE. That's what we get because of Jesus.

   That's what Jonah got.

Look at the rest of the text.

READ 3:1-2

This time Jonah went.

At last the 'dove' is flying the right way!
    This time he does not listen to his fears and his prejudices.
    Instead he takes his cue from the WORD OF THE LORD.

And what about us?
Which way are we headed this morning?

    We don't really need fresh orders, do we?
    The first set is still in effect:
        MAKE DISCIPLES.   WIN THE LOST!   PREACH THE WORD!

And what a word we have to preach!
    Not that somber warning Jonah gave Nineveh:
        Yet 40 days and Nineveh shall be overthrown

    but rather
        To you this day a Savior – Christ the Lord!

This morning I preach that message into your ears.
    In this season of lent, I repeat His call to REPENT.

    Stop running the other way.

    Instead of going the wrong way, go God's way. All the way!

    Let's accept His amnesty.
        Return from being AWOL.
            Report for duty.

        The message must be delivered.

THE LITTLE THINGS
Micah 6:6-8

READ THE TEXT

A young woman, married for ten years, sat in the counselor's office.

With tearful eyes, she anguished about the deterioration of her
marriage.
   "My husband doesn't understand," she told the counselor,
   "how much little things mean to me.

   He buys me expensive gifts...and once a year he takes me to
   a ski resort. But in between, there's nothing!

   He doesn't hold the door for me the way he used to.
   He won't help me clean off the dinner table.
   He never thanks me for a meal, or tells me I look pretty.

      All these little things are killing our relationship."

You know it as well as she. LITTLE THINGS MEAN A LOT!

Not only in marriage, but in every one of life's relationships.
   Common courtesies like a thank-you note,
      a few moments spent helping in a tedious task,
         or some patient listening even when other duties call.

For in between the MOMENTOUS occasions of life – the birthdays, the
   anniversaries, the weddings and graduations –
   there are a lot of ORDINARY DAYS
      filled with those little things that mean so much.

The poet William Wordsworth went so far as to call it
   The best portion of a good man's life – the little, nameless
   unremembered acts of kindness and of love.

259

The Bible tells us that God also cares about the little things.

Long ago He gave the prophet Micah a list of what He expects from us. A deceptively simple list of 'little things':

He has shown you, O man, what is good; and what does the Lord require of you but to do justice
                    and to love kindness
                    and to walk humbly with your God?

DO JUSTICE! God says.

The words of this great verse (Micah 6:8) are engraved in stone on the Supreme Court Building in Washington, D. C.

Justice was important 2700 years ago, and it is still important NOW!

Justice is the ordering and maintaining of proper and honest relationships with our fellow man.

We all expect our leaders to live and act justly.
    We expect honesty. We want integrity.
    Creeds and deeds in sync.

We're rightly distressed to discover
    South Carolina's governor lying about an affair with a woman in South America,
        or an Illinois police chief taking bribes from criminals.

We expect our leaders to do the RIGHT thing, the JUST thing.

But does God expect any LESS from the rest of us?

I'm not thinking of lofty matters, but of the most ordinary things.
Of honesty and fair dealing in everyday relationships.

God has His eye on the 'little, nameless, unremembered acts' by which
we treat each other fairly or unfairly -
> whether or not we fill in our tax forms honestly
> whether or not we do a thorough job for a customer,
>> even if the customer won't know the difference,
> whether or not we tell the store clerk she gave us
>> too much change.

Would you say those are LITTLE THINGS?

Perhaps so, but they mean much to God.   He says **Do justice!**

To this He adds a second little thing: **Love kindness**!

God's people are called to be KIND:

> When I was a student at Concordia Sr. College in Ft. Wayne,
>> there was a woman who came each day to the reflecting pond
>> to feed the ducks.

>> How they scurried quacking toward her when she appeared!
>> We called her the Duck Lady.

>> Nobody paid her to do it. She just had a kind heart for them.

Yes, we are to be KIND to animals.
> But how much more to PEOPLE, who are made in the image of God!

> Real kindness is the sort given to people who never say thanks,
> and may not even deserve it!

> I will never forget the day
> my FATHER went out of his way to escort a drunk driver home.

>> On the way he flashed his lights at oncoming cars to warn them
>> to be careful.

261

At one intersection he got out of the car, went up, and told the
drunk driver that he was going to follow him home
to make sure he got there safely.

When at last the man reached his driveway
and got out of his car,
    I remember how he turned and cursed at my father.

Dad took it quietly. He drove home
without comment or complaint.

My father got no award.
The incident did not make the newspaper.

But it made a mighty impression on me!

Such kindnesses keep our world from falling apart.
It has happened to you, hasn't it?
    The fellow who stopped to help you change a tire in the rain.
        The nurse in the emergency room who smiled and calmed you
        down.
            The neighbor who found your missing dog and brought him
            back to you.

God loves KINDNESS. Especially in the little things.

Do we?

The prophet Micah spoke these words to an audience of people who
had failed miserably at both JUSTICE and KINDNESS.
    They were outwardly religious, but their religion was only skin
    deep, a thin whitewash that covered a selfish, greedy lifestyle.

What about US?
    We think of our church as a FRIENDLY church.
        Are we each doing our part to make it so
        for people who visit on a Sunday?

And what of our GROUPS -
   our youth group, adult choir, women's guild, and boards?

   How do we treat one another – speak about one another –
   when our backs are turned?

Friend, what does this passage say to you personally?

   Someone said, "Character is the way we act when we think no
   one is looking."
      When no one is watching you, are you just? truthful? kind?

   As I hear this passage, I remember times when I was not kind at all,
   but ill-tempered and rude -
      times when I did helpful things, but with clenched teeth,
      despising how someone lived or even looked!

   I remember times when I was not just –
      when I ducked my responsibilities,
      or lied to cover my tracks.

Look carefully into the mirror of God's Word, friend.
   Do you see such things in yourself?

If so, what can we DO?

Micah's audience had the idea that a heavy dose of religion
   would offset any lack of personal integrity.

   They said, "Give God some RELIGION! That's what He likes.
      Worship services! Large sacrifices!"

   Shall I come before him with burnt offerings?
   Will the Lord be pleased with thousands of rams,
      with 10,000s of rivers of oil?

People still do that.

In the church I served in Akron, Ohio, there was a man
who never came to church,
   but regularly sent in a large check.

Members of his family expressed concern that he was living
a morally questionable life. They worried about him.

One night I went to visit him. I attempted to invite him back to
church and to living an upright, godly life.
   He was non-committal about both.

But as I was leaving, he followed me to the car.
Through my open window he thrust a $100 bill.

Is that what it takes? Some great thing?   A BIG OFFERING?

How much, do you suppose, would it actually cost to pay the debt we
owe God?
   $100? $1000?   More....?

Shall I, Micah asks, **give my firstborn for my transgression,
the fruit of my body for the sin of my soul?**

No, says the Lord. NO.

I have already done that great thing!
   Already I have given my firstborn, my only-begotten Son.

The great thing, that sacrifice of blood,
I have already done for you.

But there is one more LITTLE THING I ask of you...

Walk humbly with your God.
   There is no other way for sinful people to walk.
   It must be HUMBLY.

264

Aware that everything I would dare bring God was not mine at
all, but HIS already!

Humbly.
Aware that I can bring Him nothing but my sins
and ask Him for pardon.

WALK HUMBLY WITH ME, says God, and I will show you....
NO! I will give you that kindness and that justice I require from you.

When Jesus came, there came with Him both JUSTICE and KINDNESS
from God...
Justice? He kept the Law as we could not.
Kindness? He showed such love as none could have dared imagine.

By His death he paid our debt, and Justice was satisfied.

What a WONDER that God would do such things for us!

WALK HUMBLY, then. Walk humbly with your God.

Ask that Jesus come and live inside of you in all these ordinary days
and work in you to do those LITTLE THINGS
that matter so much.

Those who live that way are transformed, and they in turn transform
their world.

Booker T. Washington, the famous black educator who was also
a humble believer in Christ, took over the presidency of Tuskegee
Institute in Alabama many years ago.

One afternoon he was walking through an all-white neighborhood
in the city
when he was stopped by a wealthy white woman.

Not knowing Mr. Washington by sight, she called him over and asked him if he would like
to earn a few dollars by chopping wood.

Washington rolled up his sleeves and proceeded to do the work she asked.
After he had carried it into the house, he declined the money and went on his way.

But a neighbor girl recognized him and ran to tell the woman who it was
that had chopped her wood.

Frightfully embarrassed, the woman went the next day to Booker T. Washington's office at the Institute and apologized profusely.

But he replied gently,
"It's all right. I enjoy physical labor now and then. Besides, it is a delight to do something for a friend."

A LITTLE THING, was it?   Perhaps.

But it is in the little things that God is often at work.

It was with little things – a manger and a cross – that He redeemed us.

It is in little things – water, bread and wine, spoken words, and the neighbor in need – that He comes to us now.

And it is with little things – those 'little, nameless, unremembered acts of kindness and of love' –
that we may make this sad world REJOICE!

Dear brother, dear sister, **What does the Lord require of you
but to do justice and to love kindness
and to walk humbly with your God?**

266

A MESSAGE FOR LIARS
Zephaniah 3:9-13

_____

This will startle you, but I must say it: YOU ARE A LIAR!

And now something equally startling:
   I AM A LIAR TOO, a liar like all the rest of you!

I can still recall the day I tried to deceive my fifth grade teacher.

   Mrs. Abdon had made a social studies assignment.
      We were supposed to write a story about taking a trip to New
      York with details about how we would make the journey.
         It would display our familiarity with methods of travel and
         with geography.

   I had forgotten. I had written nothing.

   The dreadful realization hit me when she asked me to come
      forward and read my paper to the class!

   Did I admit my forgetfulness?
   NO! Instead I fished through my desk, gathered some blank sheets
      of paper, and came forward with my mind working furiously.

   Facing the class, I began to 'read' my non-existent assignment.

   I got as far as Pittsburgh
      when Mrs. Abdon walked behind me and looked
      at the blank sheets.

      I'll never forget what she said:
         "Why, Michael Kasting, you've been deceiving me!"

   I hung my head and walked back to my seat in shame.

267

I wish I could say I learned my lesson and told the truth from then on.
   But it was not so.

I have continued to struggle with telling the truth, right up to
   the present time.

In pondering this message for liars, I was reminded of some lies that
I have told just in the past few years,
      while serving as your pastor.

      A lie to a parishioner about being sick when I wasn't.
      A lie to a brother pastor to explain away my absence at
         a prayer breakfast.

      In both cases, my conscience went to work.
      I confessed the lies,
         and those brothers forgave me.

      But the awful truth remains. I still struggle with lying.

The reason for all this finger-pointing at myself, and at you, is today's
Old Testament lesson.
   Call it 'An Inconvenient Truth from an Obscure Prophet'!

Zephaniah may be an obscure ancient prophet, but his message
   is desperately relevant in our culture of deception.

Hear him well! He tells God's truth:
   **Then I will purify the lips of the peoples, that all of them may
   call on the name of the Lord and serve Him shoulder to
   shoulder... On that day, you will not be put to shame for all
   the wrongs you have done to me, because I will remove from
   this city those who rejoice in their pride. Never again will you
   be haughty on my holy hill. But I will leave within you the
   meek and the humble, who trust in the name of the Lord. The
   remnant of Israel will do no wrong; they will SPEAK NO LIES,
   Nor will deceit be found in their mouths.**

These days we are lied to so often
   that we no longer know whom we can believe.

   Whom do YOU believe?
      The President of the USA?
         The editor of our local newspaper?
         The principal of our high school?

   The National Opinion Research Center at the University of Chicago
      showed that the percentage of those who are confident about
      what they hear from financial institutions at 28%,
                    teachers at 27%,
                 organized religion at 24%
                and the press at 19%.

   Our legal system must employ lie detectors and levy stiff penalties
   for perjury
      because lying is such a common phenomenon, even when
      people are under oath!

I think most of us would agree
   that lying is a very serious problem 'out there' in our nation.

   The hard part of this sermon will be to accept the very first
   sentences I spoke:

   That YOU AND I ARE LIARS TOO!

   It's like driving at night.
      How easy to see that the other guy has his brights on.
      How easy to forget our own headlights
         until the other fellow blinks at us!

Some of us, no doubt, are <u>bigger</u> liars than others,
   or more <u>frequent</u> liars.
   But I doubt that we would find anyone who consistently tells
      'the truth, the whole truth, and nothing but the truth'!

Researchers in Massachusetts tracked ordinary conversations
and discovered that 60% of people
lied at least once in the course of a 10-minute conversation.
Most of them lied 2 or 3 times.

One psychologist estimated that the average NORMAL person lies,
on average, three times a day –
that's over a thousand times a year!

We needn't quibble over statistics.
Can we simply admit that we have this problem?

If so, then we will find Zephaniah's message both urgent
and helpful.

First, the URGENT part. Liar, your problem is serious!

Serious because it angers GOD.
Proverbs 6 mentions seven things God hates – among them are
a 'lying tongue' and a 'false witness.'

St. Paul lists lying right alongside murder and adultery as terrible
wrongdoing.

Lying is an affront to God because GOD IS TRUTH.
God is not a man that he should lie (Numbers 23:19).

Lies, in fact, originate with the Devil, whom Jesus called
a liar from the beginning...the father of lies (John 8:44).

This sin is serious for another reason. IT DESTROYS PEOPLE.

Most of us have grown so accustomed to the lying that goes on
around us that we forget the frightful consequences:
Businesses ruined.   Employees fired.
Marriages undermined.   Congregations split.

All because someone lied.
And someone else believed it, and passed it on!

We like to excuse our lies.
  "I was just trying to make her feel better"
    "It's such a little thing...it won't matter"

We're not LYING!   No, we are merely
  "stretching the truth"
    "fibbing"
      "exaggerating a little."

But Zephaniah pulls us up short. Here's what's really going on, he says earlier in chapter 3:

Woe to...the oppressing city. Her officials within her are roaring lions; her judges are ravening wolves...her prophets are wanton, faithless men!

In short, the people's tongues have become weapons of violence.

Therefore, Zephaniah announced most urgently of all,
  A DAY OF WRATH IS COMING!

A day of distress and anguish he says in chapter one,
A day of ruin and devastation...of darkness and gloom...of trumpet blast and battle cry.

On that day, says our text,
  God will remove those haughty folks with impure speech
  and leave only those humble people who tell no lies!

Am I speaking of Judgment Day?
  YES! That day is sure to come!
  The day we give account for "every careless word."
  But God's wrath will catch up with some liars long before then!

    Remember Ananias and Sapphira in the Book of Acts?

They were struck dead in their tracks for lying to the apostles about a donation to the church!

Their deaths put the fear of God into the early believers.

Remember, more recently, Presidents Nixon and Clinton, both caught lying to the American people.
Clinton lied under oath about his relationship with Monica Lewinsky and subsequently became the second president in U.S. history to be impeached by the House of Representatives.

So I say these words of the prophet are URGENT words to be taken to heart.
A day of WRATH ON LIARS IS COMING!

But that is only part of Zephaniah's message, and not yet the most Important part.

Hear a second part – a helpful, hopeful side of his message:
THERE IS HELP FOR LIARS!

In the movie *LIAR, LIAR*,
Jim Carrey plays a habitually dishonest lawyer who, for 24 hours, is UNABLE to tell a lie because of a wish his son has made.

It is hilarious (and fascinating!) to see the difference that is made when he begins at last to tell the truth on a consistent basis.

But the movie cure won't work.
People don't become truthful because we WISH it were so.
Something more is needed.

Zephaniah announces it. God has made a determination:
At that time I will change the speech of all peoples to a pure speech.

272

Please note the SUBJECT of that sentence!
It is not WE who change our speech. God does it.

This sermon is not a moralistic plug for everyone to stop lying and
try harder to tell the truth.

Instead, I announce that God will act decisively to change us.

Please also note the OBJECT.
It is not the MOUTH God will change,
but the SPEECH that comes out of it.

Some of us, by the way, may remember getting our mouths washed
out with soap…
possibly several times!

God's cleansing goes deeper.
He knows it is not the mouth but the PERSON HIMSELF that
needs changing.

If we are to have clean mouths,
we must be made clean on the inside.

So clean will we be, says the prophet in verse 11, that
on that day you will not be put to shame
but shall stand before God with consciences completely
unburdened.

There is only one person who can so completely change the heart,
cleanse the mouth,
and unburden the guilty conscience,
leaving us unashamed in God's presence…

That is JESUS CHRIST. **I am the Truth,** He said.

When He came, He told people the truth,
and many of them found that, instead of crushing them,

His truth freed them to face themselves and God again.

When He came, he lived the truth that God loves and forgives liars like us.

Some people tried to use lies to stop Him.

They hired liars for His trial before Caiaphas,
   but they only made fools of themselves because
   their testimony did not agree.

And none of those lies stopped him from doing what He
came to do - to give His life freely for all those liars,
   and for us.

Experts on lying, by the way, say that those are the two biggest
Reasons why people nowadays tell lies:
   First, because they FEAR being found out.
   Second, because they hunger for ACCEPTANCE.

Hasn't Jesus taken care of both concerns?

God has already found us out.
In Christ He has washed us clean in heart and mouth,
   Canceled our guilt, forgiven us completely!   Why lie?

God has already accepted me 'just as I am'!

Why lie?

How is it with you?
   Do you catch yourself telling the old lies and half-truths
   because you are still afraid, or insecure?

Listen! God has plans for you, says Zephaniah.
   Find your refuge in the name of the Lord and He will
   change your speech.

Come to Him with an honest confession, grab hold of His mercy, and He will do the rest.

A woman once came to an evangelist and said,
"I am deeply troubled about something. I have this habit of exaggerating things. I start to tell someone something, but then I enlarge things until they are no longer believable. People no longer trust me. Can you help me, please?"

The evangelist looked at her a moment, then said,
"Let's talk to the Lord about it."

They bowed their heads and she began to pray,
"O God, thou knowest I have a slight tendency to exaggerate..."

At that point the evangelist interrupted her.
"Call it lying, madam, and he may be able to help you!"

The prophet has delivered his message for LIARS.

Let us apply it to ourselves.

Let us stop making excuses
and calling our lies by other names.

Let us be HONEST TO GOD...
and through Jesus Christ He will enable us to be honest to others.

CPSIA information can be obtained
at www.ICGtesting.com
Printed in the USA
FFOW02n1010030614
5658FF

9 781618 637871